SPREADSHEETS
Practical Models and Assignments

Gerard Morgan

GILL & MACMILLAN

Published in Ireland by
Gill & Macmillan Ltd
Goldenbridge
Dublin 8
with associated companies throughout the world

© Gerard Morgan 1994
0 7171 2161 5
Designed by Elaine Shiels, Bantry, Co. Cork
Print origination by Seton Music Graphics Ltd, Bantry, Co. Cork
Printed in Ireland by ColourBooks Ltd, Dublin

All rights reserved. No part of this publication may be
reproduced, copied or transmitted in any form or by any
means without written permission of the publishers or else
under the terms of any licence permitting limited copying
issued by the Irish Copyright Licensing Agency,
Irish Writers' Centre, Parnell Square, Dublin 1.

For my parents,
Charles and Rena Morgan

Contents

SECTION 1: BEGINNERS' LEVEL

An Introduction to Spreadsheets	1
Creating the spreadsheet	3
Basic spreadsheet functions	3
Standard facilities of a computer spreadsheet program	9
Simple invoice	10
Trading profit and loss account	12
Spreadsheet assignments—beginners' level	14

SECTION 2: INTERMEDIATE LEVEL

An Introduction to the 'Logical If' Function	26
Invoicing	27
Creating the model	28
Design and documentation of a spreadsheet	29
Example of design and documentation	30
Personal tax calculations for the year	38
Spreadsheet assignments—intermediate level	42

SECTION 3: ADVANCED LEVEL

Final Invoice Model	54
Macros	58
Automating procedures	60
Macros to accumulate balances	60
Statistics example	61
Spreadsheet assignments—advanced level	64

Appendix 1. Spreadsheet Applications, Comparisons, and Advantages and Disadvantages	77
Appendix 2. Good Spreadsheet Design Techniques: a Check-List	80
Appendix 3. Spreadsheets for Fun	81
Appendix 4. Graph Types and Examples	84
Appendix 5. The Information Technology Environment	88
Appendix 6. Glossary of Spreadsheet Terms	93

Section 1

Beginners' Level

What is a spreadsheet?

A spreadsheet is a large blank sheet made up of rows and columns, which is used for quick and easy calculation. In 1978 an American business student named Dan Bricklin got tired of adding columns of numbers, and adding them again and again when only a few changes had been made. He approached a computer programming friend to help him solve his problem. They came up with the idea of a spreadsheet called Visicalc, written for the Apple II computer.

There are many other spreadsheet programs available now. Most of these new programs contain many new features.

What does a spreadsheet look like?

	A	B	C	D	E	F	G
1		Cell B1					
2							
3							
4						Cell F4	
5							
6	Cell A6						
7							
8							
9				Cell D9			
10							
11							
12							
13							
14							
15							
16							
17							
18							
19							
20					Cell E20		
21							

Each box in the diagram on page 1 is referred to as a *cell*. Usually the *letters* identify the **columns** and the *numbers* identify the **rows**. Where row and column meet is a cell; hence cell A1 is where column A and row 1 meet, and cell B3 is where column B and row 3 meet.

A small spreadsheet could contain 200 rows and 60 columns. This would mean that it would have 12,000 cells. The size of a computer screen will not allow all these cells to be seen together. The screen can usually only show approximately six columns and twenty rows at one time.

Any movement down or across the edge of a screen will mean losing the display of some information from the previous screenful. In fact the screen can be considered as a movable window that can view only one screenful of the spreadsheet at any time.

What can be put into a spreadsheet?

Three types of item can be entered into a cell: a value, a label, or a formula.

1. Numeric or value

A value is any number on which calculations can be performed. This excludes numbers representing dates and times, numbers followed by units of measurement, and numbers at the beginning of headings. Also, large numbers must be entered without the traditional comma (or, in modern practice, the space) used as a thousand marker, as this would prevent calculations being carried out on them. Most spreadsheets, however, can *add* such markers to the values by using the number formatting facility.

2. Label

A label is any non-numeric data. It is usually textual data used as row or column headings, but could include numbers that are not used for calculation purposes. Examples of labels in the spreadsheet opposite are 'Income', 'Expenses', 'Profit', and the spreadsheet title.

3. Formula

A formula is any algebraic expression, usually used to perform calculations on different cells. For example, in cell B8 in the illustration opposite, +B5–B6 is a formula that subtracts the contents of cell B6 from the contents of cell B5. When a formula is typed into a cell, the *result* of the calculation is displayed, not the formula.

It is important to indicate clearly that you want the contents of a cell to be a formula. This is done differently in different spreadsheet programs. In Lotus 1-2-3, for example, a formula starts with one of the following symbols: +, –, (, @. In Microsoft Excel a formula must begin with the equals sign (=).

Remember to use the asterisk (*) as the multiplication sign, the stroke (/) for division, and the circumflex (^) for 'to the power of', and to leave no spaces between numbers and signs.

	A	B	C	D	E	F
1	PROFIT STATEMENT					
2						
3		Year 2	Year 3	Year 4		
4						
5	Income	10000	20000	40000		
6	Expenses	5000	8000	9000		
7		-------	-------	-------		
8	Profit	+B5-B6	+C5-C6	+D5-D6		
9		=======	=======	=======		
10						
11						

Creating the spreadsheet

- In cell A1, type the heading. This does not require you to change the column width.
- Leave cell A2 blank.
- Type the label **Year 2** in cell B3, then move to cell C3 and type in the label **Year 3**, and finally move to cell D4 and type in **Year 4**. Repeat this process for the row labels.
- Type in the numbers that do not require any calculations first. The other numbers are based on typed-in formulas.
- When typing in the formulas, remember to indicate clearly that you want the contents of a cell to be a formula. This is done differently in different spreadsheet programs.
- Note that the formula will not be displayed but the *result* of the calculation.

Basic spreadsheet functions

The following basic spreadsheet functions will be discussed in this section:

- Editing data
- Aligning labels
- Inserting rows and columns
- Changing the format of numbers
- The summation function
- 'What if?' questions
- Copying or replication

EDITING DATA

All spreadsheets allow the user to easily change the contents of any cell by using the editing facilities, such as delete, backspace, and insert. The user simply moves the pointer to the cell to be edited and types over the content or edits it.

ALIGNING LABELS

You will notice that the labels 'Year 2' etc. are not exactly in line with the amounts below them. This is because numbers are automatically displayed *flush right* or aligned on the right (i.e. the last digit is in the extreme right of the cell), whereas the text is automatically displayed *flush left* or aligned to the left (i.e. the first character of the label is in the extreme left of the cell). However, it is possible to change the alignment of any cell to flush right, flush left, or centred.

The spreadsheet will look like the illustration below after changing the year labels to flush right.

	A	B	C	D	E
1	PROFIT STATEMENT				
2					
3		Year 2	Year 3	Year 4	
4					
5	Income	10000	20000	40000	
6	Expenses	5000	8000	9000	
7		---------	---------	---------	
8	Profit	5000	12000	31000	
9		=========	=========	=========	
10					

INSERTING ROWS AND COLUMNS

It is possible to insert extra rows and columns of data into a spreadsheet. When a row is inserted, the existing rows below will be pushed down. If a column is inserted, then the existing columns to the right will be pushed over.

In this example we might want to insert a new column in column B for 'Year 1' income and expenses. We would give the appropriate command, and all the existing columns to the right of column B will move one place to the right. The formulas will also automatically change to reflect their new position; for example, the formula in cell C8 for year 2 will change to +C5–C6.

	A	B	C	D	E	F	G
1	PROFIT STATEMENT						
2							
3		Year 1	Year 2	Year 3	Year 4		
4							
5	Income	8000	10000	20000	40000		
6	Expenses	3400	5000	8000	9000		
7		---------	---------	---------	---------		
8	Profit	4600	5000	12000	31000		
9		=========	=========	=========	=========		
10							

CHANGING THE FORMAT OF NUMBERS

It is possible to change the way numbers are displayed (their *format*) on a spreadsheet.

In the example above, the numbers should be in *money format*, i.e. with a pound sign at the beginning and a comma to separate the thousands. After this command is given, the spreadsheet would look like this:

	A	B	C	D	E	F	G
1	PROFIT STATEMENT						
2							
3		Year 1	Year 2	Year 3	Year 4		
4							
5	Income	£8,000	£10,000	£20,000	£40,000		
6	Expenses	£3,400	£5,000	£8,000	£9,000		
7		----------	----------	----------	----------		
8	Profit	£4,600	£5,000	£12,000	£31,000		
9		==========	==========	==========	==========		
10							

Many other formats are available.

THE SUMMATION FUNCTION

In our example, we want to show the totals for income, expenses and profit for the four years. We will type a suitable heading in cell F3: 'Total'. The formula to total the income would be +B5+C5+D5+E5. However, we can use the 'sum' or 'total' function to add up whole columns or rows of numbers. Instead of typing all the parts of the formula, we type in the first and last cell reference of the row or column to be added. Using Microsoft Excel, cell F5 would read **=SUM(B5:E5)**. In Lotus 1-2-3 it would read **@sum(B5..E5)**.

Similarly, the formula in F6 (+B6+C6+D6+E6) would read **sum(B6:E6)** or **@sum(B6..E6)**. The formula in F8 (+B8+C8+D8+E8) would read **sum(B8:E8)** or **@sum(B8..E8)**. Check your own spreadsheet for this function.

Our spreadsheet will look like this after this change:

	A	B	C	D	E	F	G	H
1	PROFIT STATEMENT							
2								
3		Year 1	Year 2	Year 3	Year 4	Total		
4								
5	Income	£8,000	£10,000	£20,000	£40,000	£78,000		
6	Expenses	£3,400	£5,000	£8,000	£9,000	£25,400		
7		----------	----------	----------	----------	----------		
8	Profit	£4,600	£5,000	£12,000	£31,000	£52,600		
9		==========	==========	==========	==========	==========		
10								

It is possible in most spreadsheet programs to represent the information in a spreadsheet in graphic or picture form. Four examples are given for this spreadsheet. When the spreadhseet changes, the graphs automatically reflect these changes.

Bar graph of income data

Pie chart of income data

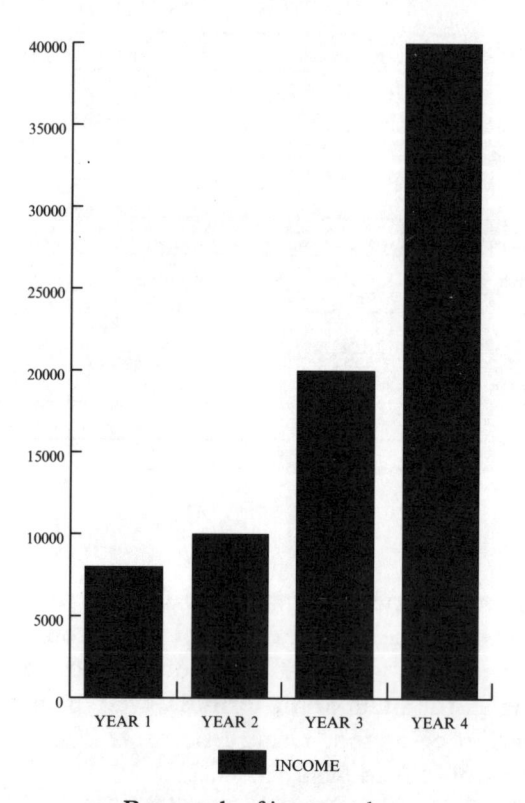

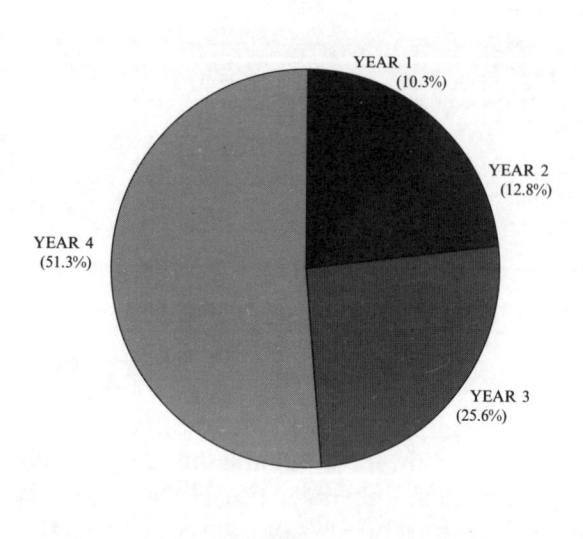

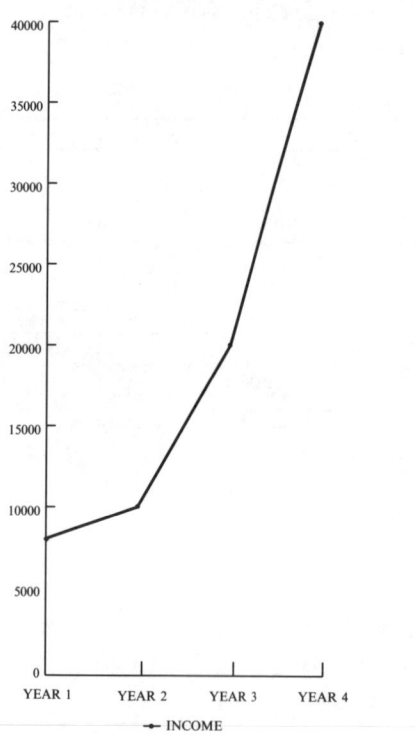

Line graph of income data

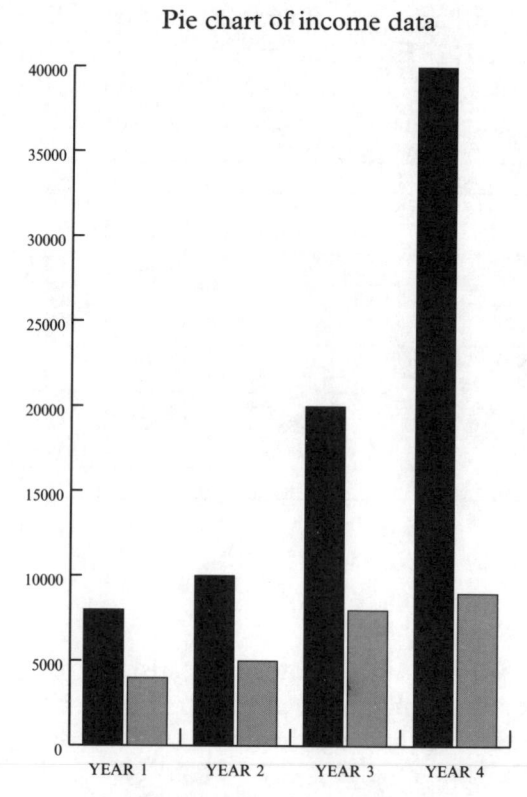

Bar graph of income and expense data

The average for the four years could also be shown; this could be put in column G. There are two ways of doing this. The formula in cell G5 for the average income over four years could be the total for the four years divided by 4 (+F5/4); or you could use the built-in average function: for example, in Lotus 1-2-3 the average function (@avg) is used exactly like the sum function: **@avg(b5..f5)**.

Our spreadsheet will look like this after the change:

	A	B	C	D	E	F	G	H
1	PROFIT STATEMENT							
2								
3		Year 1	Year 2	Year 3	Year 4	Total	Average	
4								
5	Income	£8,000	£10,000	£20,000	£40,000	£78,000	£19,500	
6	Expenses	£3,400	£5,000	£8,000	£9,000	£25,400	£6,350	
7		--------	--------	--------	--------	--------		
8	Profit	£4,600	£5,000	£12,000	£31,000	£52,600	£13,150	
9		========	========	========	========	========		
10								
11								

'WHAT IF?' ANALYSIS

When a spreadsheet is set up, we can experiment with the numbers to consider the effect of different number or policy changes. These are called *'what if?'* calculations. They are very simple to carry out on a spreadsheet already set up, because when a new number is keyed in, the spreadsheet will automatically recalculate the totals based on the new numbers.

In our example we could ask: What if the income in year 4 was only £20,000? ... How would this affect profit for that year? ... How would it affect the average income figure for the four years? ...

All these questions can be answered by keying in **20000** in cell E5. All totals and averages affected by this change will be automatically recalculated. The spreadsheet will now look like this:

	A	B	C	D	E	F	G	H
1	PROFIT STATEMENT							
2								
3		Year 1	Year 2	Year 3	Year 4	Total	Average	
4								
5	Income	£8,000	£10,000	£20,000	£20,000	£58,000	£14,500	
6	Expenses	£3,400	£5,000	£8,000	£9,000	£25,400	£6,350	
7		--------	--------	--------	--------	--------		
8	Profit	£4,600	£5,000	£12,000	£11,000	£32,600	£8,150	
9		========	========	========	========	========		
10								

This single change in cell E5 changes the figures in five other cells: F5, G5, E8, F8, and G8. It is this ability to quickly do 'what if?' analysis that makes spreadsheets extremely useful and powerful analytical tools.

COPYING OR REPLICATION

You will have noticed when typing in the example above that there is some repetitive typing of formulas. All spreadsheets allow you to copy formulas or text from one area of the spreadsheet to another.

There are three types of cell reference used when copying formulas (note that a **cell reference** means a cell address when used in a formula):

> *Absolute cell reference* — there is no change in the cell references when copied.
>
> *Relative cell reference* — the new copied formulas change cell references in accordance with their position when copied.

Absolute and relative cell reference — some cell references in the formula do not change and other cell references do change when copied.

	A	B	C	D	E
1	Absolute	Relative	Absolute-relative		
2	A1*B1	A1*B1	A1*B1		
3	A1*B1	A2*B2	A1*B2		
4	A1*B1	A3*B3	A1*B3		
5	A1*B1	A4*B4	A1*B4		
6	A1*B1	A5*B5	A1*B5		
7					

The formula to be copied is the first one in each column: all others are copied formulas. Notice that only *row numbers* change by one when copying relative cell references down a column.

	A	B	C	D	E	F
1	Absolute	A1*B1	A1*B1	A1*B1	A1*B1	
2	Relative	A1*B1	B1*C1	C1*D1	D1*E1	
3	Absolute-relative	A1*B1	A1*C1	A1*D1	A1*E1	
4						

The first formula in each row is the one to be copied: all others are copied formulas. Notice that only *column letters* change by one when copying relative cell references across a row.

In the profit statement on page 7, we could have used the 'copy' function to enter the formula in cells B8 to E8. This would be done by entering the first formula in B8 and using the 'copy' command to copy from B8 (**source cell**) to cells C8, D8, and E8 (**target cells**). The cell reference will need to change when copied; therefore we will use relative cell references for both parts of the source cell formula in B8.

It is this function that gives the computer spreadsheet real power. Once the original or source formulas have been typed in, it is only a matter of replicating them as far as the memory of your computer will allow. Spreadsheets can be constructed very quickly and easily using replication.

Standard facilities of a computer spreadsheet program

- The cursor can be moved quickly to anywhere in the spreadsheet
- Rows and columns can be inserted in existing data
- Rows, columns and ranges of data can be deleted
- Cell display can be changed to show different formats
- Single items or ranges of data can be copied
- Formulas can be copied or replicated (relative or absolute)
- Mathematical functions are available, for example 'sum', 'tan', 'average', 'sin', 'cos', etc. (and in most spreadsheets other functions are also available, such as financial and statistical functions)
- Editing facilities are available during and after the typing in of data
- Column widths can be changed
- Data can be stored for later retrieval
- Part or all of the spreadsheet can be printed
- Logical decisions can be made on data using the 'if' function
- Coded data can be looked up using the 'lookup' function
- Rows and columns can be fixed on the screen (non-scrolling titles) where more than one screenful of data is used
- Data can be protected on the spreadsheet so as to prevent changes being made
- Data-base facilities, such as sorting and searching, are available
- Graphing facilities are available, making it possible to produce bar graphs, line graphs, pie charts, etc.
- Some spreadsheets allow integration with other programs, such as graphics or word-processing programs.

Creating a spreadsheet: some guidelines

Before typing a spreadsheet into a computer you should plan out what you want to do. This will involve some of the following steps.

1. What title am I going to use in the spreadsheet?
2. What headings will I use for the rows and columns? These should be concise but descriptive.
3. Will I need to increase or decrease the width of a column, and if so, by how much?
4. Which of the items will be a label and which a numeric or value?
5. Where will I use a formula, and can I use a built-in function?
6. Can I replicate this formula? If so, will it be relative, absolute, or a combination?
7. Should the data be displayed in a special format, for example cash format, and where?
8. What file name will I use for the spreadsheet? This name will have to be concise but should remind you of the contents of the spreadsheet when retrieving it later.

Spreadsheets are extremely useful and powerful analytical tools. They are used by many different people and professions, including accountants, statisticians, engineers, and scientists. They are easy to use, and complex spreadsheets can be constructed quickly by using replication and the many built-in functions and facilities discussed.

Simple invoice

THE MODEL: EXPLANATION

This is a simple model where the user can enter data to produce an invoice. The spreadsheet is set up to perform the following functions when the data is keyed in:

- Calculate the value per line of the invoice
- Calculate the subtotal
- Calculate the discount and the amount of VAT
- Finally calculate the total due

CREATING THE MODEL

1. Make sure that column B is wide enough to accommodate the text. It should be set to at least 25 characters.
2. Change columns D to F to money format in the range D17 to F33. Do not use the 'format' command for all numbers, as not all numbers will be money amounts.
4. The date in cell B12 must be entered as a label, or changed to date format.

THE FORMULAS USED

In cell F17 the formula is **D17*E17**. This formula multiplies the unit price (D17) by the quantity (E17). This formula should be copied from cell F17 to cell F24. Notice that the cell references will change down the column, so they will be relative cell references.

In cell F26 the formula represents the sum of the range from F17 to F24 (**@sum(f17..f24)**).

In cell F27 the formula is **F26*.02**. It calculates the discount. This is done by multiplying the subtotal (F26) by the discount rate (0.02 or 2/100).

In cell F29 the formula is **F26–F27**. This subtracts the discount (F27) from the subtotal (F26).

In cell F30 the formula is **F29*.16**. It calculates the VAT. This is done by multiplying the net value (F29) by the VAT rate (0.16 or 16/100).

In cell F32 the formula is **F29+F30**.

	A	B	C	D	E	F	G
1	INVOICE						
2							
3		J. Murphy Ltd					
4		12 Castle Drive					
5		Arklow, Co. Wicklow					
6				To:	Frames Ltd		
7					21 Arklow Road		
8					Wicklow		
9	Customer	Date		Order no.	Invoice no.	Sale type	
10	account no.						
11	----------	--------------------		----------	----------	----------	
12	3434346	12/1/1994		342	654	Cash	
13	----------	--------------------		----------	----------	----------	
14							
15	Part no.	Description			Unit price	Quantity	Total price
16	----------	--------------------			----------	----------	----------
17	3422	Hacksaw			£0.70	23	£16.10
18	2333	Wooden hammer, 1 kg			£5.90	31	£182.90
19	3432	No. 8 screws, brass			£0.03	100	£3.00
20							£0.00
21							£0.00
22							£0.00
23							£0.00
24							£0.00
25							----------
26						Subtotal	£202.00
27						Discount 2%	£4.04
28							----------
29						Net value	£197.96
30						VAT @ 16%	£31.67
31							----------
32						Total due	£229.63
33							==========
34							

Trading profit and loss account

THE MODEL: EXPLANATION

The example here shows a typical trading profit and loss account for a sole trader. This account is produced at the end of a trading year; it is used to calculate the profit or loss arising from a year's trading.

The figures entered by the user are those that do not require any calculations, i.e. the actual accounting information for that year. The program should automatically compute any of the calculations to sum or deduct in order to calculate the profit by the use of formulas.

CREATING THE MODEL

The width of column A will need to be adjusted to accommodate the text (approximately 25 characters).

To show money amounts correctly, the format for the entire spreadsheet should be money format.

Formulas used

In cell E5, **D4–D5** subtracts the contents of D5 (sales returns) from D4 (sales).
In cell D11, **D8+D9** adds the contents of the two cells.
In cell E12, **D11–D12** subtracts the contents of the two cells.
In cell E17, **E14+E15** adds the contents of the two cells.
In cell C24, **B23–B24** subtracts the contents of the two cells.
In cell D25, the built-in function is used to add numbers in the range C21 to C25.
In cell D31, the built-in function is used to add numbers in the range C29 to C31.
In cell D36, the built-in function is used to add numbers in the range C34 to C36.
In cell D42, the built-in function is used to add numbers in the range C40 to C42.
In cell E42, **D25+D31+D36+D42** adds the contents of the four cells (all the subtotals for expenses).
In cell E44, **E17–E42** subtracts total expenses from gross profit.

	A	B	C	D	E	F
1	TRADING PROFIT AND LOSS ACCOUNT					
2	Year ended 31/12/1993					
3						
4	Sales			87,300		
5	Less sales returns			4,500	82,800	
6				----------		
7	Less cost of sales:					
8	Opening stock			7,000		
9	Purchases			35,000		
10						
11	Cost of goods available			42,000		
12	Less closing stock			10,000	32,000	
13				----------	----------	
14	Gross profit				50,800	
15	Add discount received				450	
16					----------	
17					51,250	
18						
19	Less expenses:					
20	Establishment:					
21	Rent and rates		1,786			
22	ESB		432			
23	Insurance	1,500				
24	Less insurance prepaid	200	1,300			
25	Deprec. office equipment	----------	659	4,177		
26			----------			
27						
28	Administration:					
29	Salaries		20,000			
30	Office expenses		569			
31	Postage		321	20,890		
32			----------			
33	Financial:					
34	Bad debts		300			
35	Discount allowed		213			
36	Bank charges		231	744		
37			----------			
38						
39	Selling and distribution:					
40	Carriage		500			
41	Motor expenses		1,000			
42	Advertising		3,700	5,200	31,011	
43			----------	----------	----------	
44	Net profit				20,239	
45					==========	
46						

'WHAT IF?' CALCULATIONS

This model could be used to see the effects that different policies would have on profit. For example, research shows that a different advertising campaign costing £15,000 would increase sales to £102,800. What effect would this have on profit? To answer the question we simply put the new figures in the appropriate cells, and the new profit will be calculated automatically (i.e. type **102800** in cell D4 and **15000** in cell C42). Would this campaign have been worth while?

Spreadsheet assignments—beginners' level

FUNCTIONS AND COMMANDS REQUIRED FOR ASSIGNMENTS

These assignments are graded, and you are advised to work through them in the order in which they are presented.

As you progress through the assignments you will discover that in order to carry out an assignment you will need to know the functions and commands specific to your spreadsheet program. You will also be practising commands and functions learnt in earlier assignments. A list of the commands required for each assignment is given below.

ASSIGNMENT 1

—Entering data into a spreadsheet, including labels and numeric data
—Changing the column width
—Changing the contents of a cell
—Deleting the contents of a cell
—Saving a spreadsheet
—Exiting the system

ASSIGNMENT 2

—Recalling a spreadsheet
—Inserting a column of data
—Justifying headings
—Formatting a block of cells to show one decimal place
—Inserting a row of data
—Saving and exiting

ASSIGNMENT 3

—Recalling a spreadsheet
—Adding a new column of data
—Adding a row ('summation' function)
—Finding the average of a row ('average' function)
—Summing a column
—Saving and exiting

ASSIGNMENT 4

All the functions above and

—'What if?' calculations

—Replicating relative cell references

—Printing

ASSIGNMENT 5

All the functions above and

—Formatting a block to display two decimal places

—Deleting a row of data

—Inserting a column of data

ASSIGNMENT 6

All the functions above and

—Manipulating formulas using brackets

ASSIGNMENT 7

As assignment 6

ASSIGNMENT 8

—Using the exponent formula ('to the power of')

ASSIGNMENT 9

As assignment 7

ASSIGNMENT 1

1. Type the following data into a spreadsheet, then make the changes listed below when you have finished.

	A	B	C	D	E	F	G	H
1	RAINFALL RECORD (mm)							
2	1/10/90							
3	All							
4	Regions	January	February	March	April	May	June	
5								
6	North	7	9	7	16	12	6	
7	West	19	16	11	11	7	3	
8	South	3	0	6	3	8	9	
9	East	7	8	9	10	5	2	
10	N-East	17	17	15	1	9	5	
11	S-East	2	2	2	12	4	5	
12	N-West	12	9	6	13	13	7	
13	S-West	7	13	15	9	14	15	
14								

2. Change the width of column A to 12 characters.
3. Change the contents of cell A10 to North-East, A11 to South-East, A12 to North-West, and A13 to South-West.
4. The rainfall figure for February for the East region was incorrectly recorded: it should have been 13 mm. Also the South-East data for June is incorrect: it should have been 15 mm. Make these adjustments.
5. Delete the contents of cell A3.
6. Your completed spreadsheet should look like the one below. Save the spreadsheet as RAIN and exit the system.

	A	B	C	D	E	F	G	H
1	RAINFALL RECORD (mm)							
2	1/10/90							
3								
4	Regions	January	February	March	April	May	June	
5								
6	North	7	9	7	16	12	6	
7	West	19	16	11	11	7	3	
8	South	3	0	6	3	8	9	
9	East	7	13	9	10	5	2	
10	North-East	17	17	15	1	9	5	
11	South-East	2	2	2	12	4	15	
12	North-West	12	9	6	13	13	7	
13	South-West	7	13	15	9	14	15	
14								

ASSIGNMENT 2

1. Recall the spreadsheet RAIN.
2. Insert a new column between 'Regions' and 'January' (at column B) containing the area of the regions (in square miles), as follows:

Regions	Area
North	4,768
West	5,674
South	3,213
East	4,356
North-East	675
South-East	567
North-West	453
South-West	689

3. You will notice that the headings 'January', 'February' etc. are not in line with the numbers. The labels are at present flush left; the numbers are flush right. Change all month labels and the heading 'Area' to be flush right.
4. Format the rainfall data in the spreadsheet to show one decimal place.

5. Insert a new row of rainfall data for **West Islands**. This should be in row 10; the present row 10 will move down to become row 11, and all other rows below this will move down automatically. The data for this region is:

Area	January	February	March	April	May	June
345	17	13	19	20	15	12

6. Your completed spreadsheet should look like the one below. Save the new spreadsheet as NEWRAIN and exit the system.

	A	B	C	D	E	F	G	H	I
1	RAINFALL RECORD (mm)								
2	1/10/1990								
3									
4	Regions	Area	January	February	March	April	May	June	
5									
6	North	4768	7.0	9.0	7.0	16.0	12.0	6.0	
7	West	5674	19.0	16.0	11.0	11.0	7.0	3.0	
8	South	3213	3.0	0.0	6.0	3.0	8.0	9.0	
9	East	4356	7.0	13.0	9.0	10.0	5.0	2.0	
10	West Islands	345	17.0	13.0	19.0	20.0	15.0	12.0	
11	North-East	675	17.0	17.0	15.0	1.0	9.0	5.0	
12	South-East	567	2.0	2.0	2.0	12.0	4.0	15.0	
13	North-West	453	12.0	9.0	6.0	13.0	13.0	7.0	
14	South-West	689	7.0	13.0	15.0	9.0	14.0	15.0	
15									
16									

ASSIGNMENT 3

1. Recall the spreadsheet NEWRAIN.
2. Add a new column after the June data to show the total rainfall for the nine regions. To do this you should use the summation function to add the data for all the regions. The heading for this column should be **Total**.
3. Add another column after the total to show the average rainfall in each region for the six months. The average will be worked out using a formula that divides the total rainfall for each region by 6. This formula will be:
    Cell with total for North ÷ 6 in new column
    Cell with total for West ÷ 6 in new column, etc.
    Call the new column 'Average', and enter the formulas.
4. In cell A16 enter the heading **Total area**. In cell B16 show the total area of all the regions. This will be done using the summation function to add the numbers in column B.
5. Change the date in cell A2 to today's date. Make sure it is a label.
6   In cell A3 enter your own name.
7. Save the spreadsheet as FINALRAIN and exit the system. Your final spreadsheet should look like the one on the next page.

	A	B	C	D	E	F	G	H	I	J	K
1	RAINFALL RECORD (mm)										
2	19/9/1994										
3	Ciara Murphy										
4	Regions	Area	January	February	March	April	May	June	Total	Average	
5											
6	North	4768	7.0	9.0	7.0	16.0	12.0	6.0	57.0	9.5	
7	West	5674	19.0	16.0	11.0	11.0	7.0	3.0	67.0	11.2	
8	South	3213	3.0	0.0	6.0	3.0	8.0	9.0	29.0	4.8	
9	East	4356	7.0	13.0	9.0	10.0	5.0	2.0	46.0	7.7	
10	West Islands	345	17.0	13.0	19.0	20.0	15.0	12.0	96.0	16.0	
11	North-East	675	17.0	17.0	15.0	1.0	9.0	5.0	64.0	10.7	
12	South-East	567	2.0	2.0	2.0	12.0	4.0	15.0	37.0	6.2	
13	North-West	453	12.0	9.0	6.0	13.0	13.0	7.0	60.0	10.0	
14	South-West	689	7.0	13.0	15.0	9.0	14.0	15.0	73.0	12.2	
15											
16	Total area	20740									
17											

ASSIGNMENT 4

This spreadsheet is used to store data about the number of trees planted in different counties. It calculates statistics based on this data.

	A	B	C	D	E	F
1	Green Trees Ltd					
2	Name					
3			NUMBER OF TREES PLANTED			
4						
5	County	Year 1	Year 2	Year 3	Year 4	
6	Wicklow	8000	10000	4110	900	
7	Kerry	9800	2000	8210	1000	
8	Mayo	400	3000	400	8000	
9	Galway	8000	4000	8000	4000	
10	Clare	400	5000	400	4000	
11	Cork	3000	4200	500	4000	
12	Waterford	3300	3210	4000	5000	
13						

1. Enter the given information into a spreadsheet, making sure that
   —all columns are set at 12 characters wide;
   —all column headings are flush right.
   Enter your name in cell A2, save the spreadsheet as TREE1, and exit the system.
2. Recall the spreadsheet TREE1, and make the following changes.
   (a) The year 2 figure for Co. Mayo is incorrect: it should be 3,820.
   (b) The year 4 figure for Co. Cork should be 4,200.
   (c) Enter today's date in cell C2.
3. Two counties have been left out; insert the information at row 9 and 10, as follows:

	Year 1	Year 2	Year 3	Year 4
Westmeath	8,000	4,000	4,000	4,000
Wexford	5,000	1,000	500	500

4. Create a new column of data in column F to show the total for four years for each county. Use a suitable column heading.
5. Create a new column of data in column G to show the average for the four years for each county. Use a suitable column heading.
6. At row 16 show the total number of trees planted in each year. Use a suitable row heading and the built-in summation function.
7. At row 17 show the average number of trees planted in each year, using the built-in average function or dividing the total number of trees for a year by 9 (the number of counties in the table). Use a suitable row heading. Show these figures to two decimal places.
8. At row 18 show the following details:

	Year 1	Year 2	Year 3	Year 4
Quota	50,000	35,000	55,000	48,000

At row 19 show the quota difference, which is calculated by subtracting the quota for that year from the total planted in the same year; for example, for year 1 the quota difference is 45,900 − 50,000 = −4,100. Copy this formula across the row. Use a suitable row heading.

9. *'What if?' calculations.* Using your set-up spreadsheet, answer the following questions.
    (*a*) If the quota for year 1 was changed to 43,000, would year 1 be above or below quota? And by how much?
    (*b*) If the number of trees planted in Co. Mayo in year 3 was 2,390 instead of 400, what would the effect be on (i) the quota difference for that year and (ii) the average number of trees planted in Co. Mayo after four years?
10. Save the spreadsheet as TREE2, and print the entire spreadsheet.

ASSIGNMENT 5

This is a spreadsheet used for keeping a record of a person's physical training during a week. The spreadsheet will allow certain calculations to be done on this data.

	A	B	C	D	E	F	G
1	CIRCUIT TRAINING RECORD						
2	For period:	3/5/92-9/5/92					
3	Name:			Exercises			
4							
5		Set-ups	Press-ups	Squats	Curls	Swings	
6	Day 1	15	20	25	30	12	
7	Day 2	4	6	8	10	12	
8	Day 3	6	6	8	6	6	
9	Day 4	2	4	6	8	9	
10	Day 5	10	15	6	15	15	
11	Day 6	2	3	20	5	9	
12	Day 7	10	12	4	3	2	
13							
14							
15							
16		Distance run	Time taken	Speed			
17		(km)	(min)	(km/h)			
18	Day 1	2.5	10.2				
19	Day 2	3.4	15				
20	Day 3	4	18				
21	Day 4	5	23				
22	Day 5	6	30				
23	Day 6	7	41.89				
24	Day 7	9	50.99				
25							

1. Set up the given spreadsheet, making sure that
   —all columns are set at 12 characters wide;
   —all column headings are flush right.
   Enter your name in cell B3, save the spreadsheet as CIRC1, and print it.
2. Make the following changes.
   (a) The number of press-ups for day 6 is incorrect: it should be 8.
   (b) Curls for day 2 should be 13.
   (c) Change the heading in cell B5 to 'Sit-ups'.
3. (a) Enter a formula in cell B14 to total all sit-up exercises for the week (use the 'sum' function).
   (b) Copy this formula to cells C14 to E14 to show totals for the other four exercises. Use a suitable row heading.
4. Enter a formula in cell B15 to show the average for each exercise for the week. Use a suitable row heading. Show the figures to two decimal places.
5. An exercise has been left out. Insert the exercise at column E to show the following:

	Jumps
Day 1	20
Day 2	14
Day 3	8
Day 4	6
Day 5	14
Day 6	20
Day 7	25

   Make sure you show totals and the average for this new column.
6. Use a formula in cell D18 to show the speed (in kilometres per hour) for each day. This is calculated by dividing the time taken (in minutes) into the distance run and multiplying this by 60; for example for day 1, km/h = **(2.5/10.2)*60** = 14.7058. Copy this formula down the column to show the speed for each day. Show all speeds to two decimal places.
7. (a) In cell D25 show the average speed for the week. Use a suitable heading.
   (b) In cell B25 show the total distance travelled in the week. Use a suitable heading.
8. *'What if?' calculations.* Use your set-up spreadsheet to answer the following questions.
   (a) How many extra squats must the athlete do on day 4 to double his or her weekly average? (Do this by experimenting with different numbers of squats for day 4 to see how this affects the weekly average.)
   (b) If the distance run on day 6 was 7.94 km, what would the speed be for that day, and how much will the average speed for the week change because of this?
9. Save the spreadsheet as CIRC2, and print the entire spreadsheet.

Assignment 6

1. Set up the spreadsheet given in the example to produce the trading profit and loss account as given in this section.
2. In an appropriate part of the spreadsheet, show the following analysis figures for any trading profit and loss figures. Use suitable headings.

Profitability analysis

These figures indicate how profitable the company is. The higher the percentages, the better for the company, for the first two percentages. The lower the ratio of expenses to sales, the better.

   Gross profit (%) = gross profit × 100 ÷ (sales – sales returns)
   Net profit (%) = net profit × 100 ÷ (sales – sales returns)
   Expenses to sales = total expenses × 100 ÷ sales

Efficiency ratio

This figure gives a measure of how many times the stock was turned over. A measure of 5 or over is considered acceptable.

Stock turnover = cost of goods available ÷ ((closing stock + opening stock) ÷ 2)

3. 'What if?' calculations.
   (a) Keeping all other figures as above, what would the sales figure need to be to have a profit of £40,000?
   (b) What would the sales figure need to be to give a gross profit percentage of 70%?
   (c) What would the sales figure need to be to give a net profit percentage of 50%?
4. Type in the new figures for the year ended 31 December 1993 and find the new profit or loss figure and ratios. The new figures are:

   Sales: £90,000
   Returns: £6,200
   Opening stock: £9,200
   Purchases: £41,000
   Closing stock: £8,000
   Discount received: £67
   Rent: £2,000
   ESB: £500
   Insurance: £2,000
   Insurance prepaid: £240
   Depreciation: £900
   Salaries: £35,000
   Office expenses: £600
   Postage: £400
   Bad debts: £200
   Discount allowed: £345
   Bank charges: £987
   Carriage: £210
   Motor expenses: £2,645
   Advertising: £5,800

5. Save the final spreadsheet as P/L.

ASSIGNMENT 7

1. Set up a spreadsheet to show cash flows over a six-month period for Beetle Garages Ltd. The cash flow statement shows all receipts (incomes) and all payments of the business. Use the following grid to set up the spreadsheet:

	January	February	March	April	May	June	Total
Receipts:							
Opening bal.	0.00						
Cash sales							
Credit sales							
Loans							
Grants							
Capital							
Total receipts (A) (per month)							
Payments:							
Rent							
Electricity							
Loan interest							
Motor parts							
Wages							
Total payments (B) (per month)							
Net cash (A – B)							

Note that the 'net cash' in January will be the opening balance in February, and the 'net cash' in February will be the opening balance in March, and so on.

2. Enter the following information into the set-up spreadsheet:

   Cash sales: £600 for the first three months, and £200 for the last three months

   Credit sales:
	Jan.	Feb.	Mar.	Apr.	May	Jun.
	£2,000	£3,000	£8,800	£600	£9,000	£1,900

   Loans:
	Jan.		Mar.			Jun.
	£4,500		£9,000			£3,000

   Grant: £3,000 in January only

   Capital: £20,000 in January only

   Rent: £400 per month

   Electricity:
	Jan.			Apr.		Jun.
	£299			£345		£235

   Loan repayment: £200 per month

   Motor parts:
	Jan.			Apr.		Jun.
	£345			£456		£277

   Wages: £1,398 per month

3. *'What if?' calculations.*
   (a) If the electricity bills were reduced to £100 every two months, what saving would this give the company?
   (b) If only £10,000 was invested in capital, would the company have a positive net cash figure in June?
4. Save the spreadsheet as CASHFLOW, and print the row headings and totals only.

ASSIGNMENT 8

In mathematics, **functions** are often used. A function is any expression that contains only one variable, for example $f(x) = x^2 - 8x + 5$.

The f stands for 'function'. The value of $f(x)$ depends on the value of x.
Thus $f(2) = 2.2 - 8.2 + 5 = -7$. So when $x = 2$, $f(x)$ is -7.

To clarify how a function operates, it is usual to show a table for $f(x)$ for several values of x.

x	-3	-2	-1	0	1	2	3	4
x^2	9	4	1	0	1	4	9	16
$-8x$	24	16	8	0	-8	-16	-24	-32
$+5$	5	5	5	5	5	5	5	5
$f(x)$	38	25	14	5	-2	-7	-10	-11

1. Set up a spreadsheet to tabulate the following functions for values of x between -3 and $+6$, inclusive, using appropriate headings, formulas, and replication. Remember that the symbol for 'to the power of' is the circumflex (^).

   $f(x) = 2x^2 + 6x - 12$ Save this table as TABLE1.
   $f(x) = 4x^3 - 3x^2 + 3x - 4$ Save this table as TABLE2.
   $f(x) = x3 - 3x^2 - 10x + 4$ Save this table as TABLE3.
   $f(x) = x5 - 4x^3 - 6x^2 - 9x - 17$ Save this table as TABLE4.

ASSIGNMENT 9

The following is a stock record spreadsheet for Annerex Ltd, who sell a range of garden products.

Product	Unit price	Fixed costs	Holding cost per unit	Number of days to deliver
Brush	4.55	20	3	12
Spade	23.99	20	5	14
Mower	45.00	39	4	7

Sales (units)

Product	Jun.	Jul.	Aug.	Sep.	Oct.	Nov.	Dec.
Brush	34	55	77	23	13	22	11
Spade	4	3	7	88	3	2	33
Mower	45	33	66	77	22	8	3

1. Show the following information for all the products:
   (a) Total annual sales in units for each product. (Use the summation function to add the rows.)
   (b) Total annual revenue for each product.
   Total annual sales revenue = total annual sales in units × unit price of the product
   (c) Total sales in units for each month. (Use the summation function to add the columns.)
   (d) Average daily demand in units, assuming 250 working days for each product.
   Average daily demand for a product = total annual sales in units ÷ 250
   (e) The minimum reorder level for each product. This level gives the company an indication of when to reorder the product: when the number of products in store reaches this level, the product should be ordered. It is based on the following formula:
   Minimum reorder level = 2 × average daily demand × number of days to deliver
   (f) The economic order quantity (EOQ) for each product, using the following formula:
   EOQ = 2 (F)(S) ÷ C
   where F is the fixed cost of placing and receiving an order, S is the annual sales in units, and C is the holding cost per unit.
2. 'What if?' calculation. If the sale of spades for June was 44, how would this affect the minimum reorder level and the economic order quantity for this product?

SECTION 2

Intermediate Level

Is the profit this year greater than last year? Has the aeroplane been overloaded with luggage? The answer to such questions is either true or false. It is considered a logical question, i.e. one having a true or false answer.

Most spreadsheet programs allow the user to use a formula to ask a question (*condition*) and generate a true or false response. The general form this formula takes is IF(*condition, action if true, action if false*). This function is very similar to the 'if—then—else' command in the programming language Basic. The following examples illustrate how it works.

EXAMPLE 1

| If age greater than 18 | entitled to vote | not entitled to vote |
| (condition) | (true) | (false) |

EXAMPLE 2

	A	B	C	D
1		GREATER NUMBER		
2	4	7	7	
3	6	4	6	
4	8	5	8	
5	9	10	10	
6	10	100	100	
7	999	900	999	
8	84	1	84	
9	100	3,000	3,000	
10				

Given the numbers in column A and B above, we want to set up a new column C to display the greater of the two numbers. To do this we must get the program to ask a question: is the number in column A greater than the number in column B (the condition)? We want to enter the bigger number into column C.

If the answer to the question is true (if the number in column A is greater), then we will enter a copy of the number in column A into column C. Otherwise (if the answer is false and the column B number is bigger), the contents of column B must be greater and should be entered in column C.

The condition entered into cell C3, in formula form, would read:

IF A3>B3   A3   B3
(condition) (true)   (false)

The meaning of this formula is: if the contents of A3 are greater than the contents of B3, then display the contents of A3 in cell C3, otherwise display the contents of B3 in cell C3. This formula would be copied down column C using relative cell references.

This function will be used in examples that follow.

RELATIONAL OPERATORS

A condition in an 'if' statement can have the following comparisons:

=	equal to
>	greater than
<	less than
>=	greater than or equal to
<=	less than or equal to
<>	not equal to

LOGICAL OPERATORS

Several conditions can be combined. This is done by using any of the following formulas:

and   both condition 1 *and* condition 2;
               for example: **IF A45 > 45 and S67 < 56 then true false**
or   either condition 1 *or* condition 2;
               for example: **IF A45 > 45 or S67 < 56 then true false**
and not   condition 1 *and not* condition 2;
               for example: **IF A45 > 45 and not S67 < 56 then true false**

Invoicing

THE MODEL: EXPLANATION

This is an extension of the simple invoice model. It allows for more detail and is more realistic. The design features are also more flexible.

The following additional features are allowed:

- Variable VAT rates
- VAT code entry
- Automatic categorising of amounts net of VAT
- Calculation of VAT

CREATING THE MODEL

1. Use input variables for the VAT percentage and discount percentage, as these should be changeable. References should be made to the cell references where these percentage rates are on the spreadsheet, rather than having fixed numbers in formulas. The cells should be in percentage format.
2. Column F is set up to show the VAT code. This is then used to categorise goods. This information will be useful when filling in the VAT3 form, which is used to show VAT amounts on sales and purchases and must be filled in every two months and sent to the Revenue Commissioners.

FORMULAS USED

The 'if' function is used to categorise the goods. (Note that no VAT is calculated yet: this is done when all categorisation is complete.) The formula in cell G21 is **IF F21="B" D21*E21 0**

IF	The 'logical if' function is being used.
F21="B"	This is the condition: that the VAT code is equal to 'B'.
D21*E21	True response: if the condition is true, place the number from this calculation (D21 × E21) in cell G21.
0	False response: if the condition is untrue, put 0 into cell G21.

This formula is copied down the column (from G21 to G28), using relative cell references. The formula in cell H21 is similar to that in G21, except for the condition:

> **IF F21="C" D21*E21 0**

In cells G34 and H34 the VAT calculation refers back to the variable VAT rates in E15 and F15. This is a good design feature, as it allows for changes in the VAT rate without changing formulas.

	A	B	C	D	E	F	G	H	I
1	INVOICE								
2									
3		J. Murphy Ltd							
4		12 Castle Drive							
5		Arklow, Co. Wicklow							
6					To:	Frames Ltd			
7						21 Arklow Road			
8						Wicklow			
9									
10	Customer	Date		Order no.	Invoice no.	Sale type			
11	account no.								
12	----------	----------		----------	----------	----------	----------	----------	
13	3434346	12/1/93		342	654	12.50%	16.00%	Cash	
14	----------	----------		----------	----------	----------	----------	----------	
15									
16	Part no.	Description			Unit price	Quantity	VAT code	Goods @ 12.5	Goods @ 16.5
17	----------	----------		----------	----------	----------	----------	----------	
18	3422	Hacksaw			£0.70	23	B	£16.10	£0.00
19	3333	Wooden hammer, 1 kg			£5.90	31	C	£0.00	£182.90
20	1233	Plasterboard, 2 by 5 m			£32.00	5	B	£160.00	£0.00
21	4425	Nails, 150 mm			£0.30	100	B	£30.00	£0.00
22								£0.00	£0.00
23								£0.00	£0.00
24								£0.00	£0.00
25								£0.00	£0.00
26								----------	----------
27					Subtotal			£206.10	182.9
28					Discount		2.00%	£4.12	£3.66
29								----------	----------
30					Net value			£201.98	£179.24
31					VAT @ 12.5 and 16.5%			25.24725	28.67872
32					Totals			£227.23	£207.92
33									
34								----------	
35					Total due			£435.15	
36								==========	
37									

Design and documentation of a spreadsheet

It is essential when you are producing a spreadsheet that it be designed in advance and that the final design be well documented (explained). This is good practice, for the following reasons.

1. It forces the designer to work logically through the design of a spreadsheet before using the computer.
2. It makes it easier to change in the future, as every aspect of the spreadsheet is explained.
3. It gives instructions for non-technical users.
4. Test data can be used to test the spreadsheet.
5. Formulas are explained.

The design specification should include:
1. *Objectives of the spreadsheet.* What the spreadsheet is trying to achieve.
2. *Input and output format.* What the form of the input and output data will be.
3. *Data-processing formulas.* The formulas used in the spreadsheet and their explanation.
4. *Protected data.* This is the area of the spreadsheet that should be protected against users overwriting important formulas or data.
5. *Data entry form.* This form will make possible the more efficient collection of data in a form usable directly from paper to the spreadsheet.
6. *Test data.* This is a constructed set of input data used to test the spreadsheet for errors. It should include data that will test formula operations; for example, if an 'if' function is used, the test data should generate a true and also a false response.
7. *Expected output (manually calculated).* The expected output when the test data is used. This should be done manually and checked against the answers in the computer spreadsheet.
8. *Spreadsheet print-out.* An exact print-out of the entire spreadsheet.
9. *Cell print-out.* A cell-by-cell print-out of the cell contents (formulas).
10. *User instructions.* These should show:
    - How to access the program
    - How to access the file
    - How and where to enter the data
    - Saving the file
    - Printing

Example of design and documentation

FLIGHT REGISTER

A small airline operates a twelve-seater aeroplane between Galway and Sligo. It wants to store passenger information in a spreadsheet. The following conditions apply:

- The basic price of a ticket is £50.
- There is VAT at 21 per cent on the basic price of all tickets (excluding discount).
- There is a 10 per cent discount on the basic price of all tickets for children under twelve.
- A passenger is charged an extra £1 for every 1 kg over the 20 kg luggage allowance. No VAT is charged on this extra amount.

The only items to be typed in are the passenger information and the standard data, such as ticket price, penalty charge, etc. All other figures are to be calculated by the spreadsheet through the use of formulas. This output is to include:

- Discount amount, if any
- VAT
- Penalty, if any
- Total ticket price

Design specification and documentation

1. *Objectives:*

- To create a spreadsheet that can be used many times for different flights, to record and calculate necessary flight details and prices.
- To supply data entry and report production.
- To protect data and formulas as much as possible.

2. *Input and output format* (see spreadsheet layout):

Variable data to be input (area A):
Seat number: numeric, 0 decimal places
Passenger name: alphabetic
Passenger age: numeric, 0 decimal places
Luggage weight: numeric, 2 decimal places

Data to be output (area C):
Price: currency, 2 decimal places
Discount: currency, 2 decimal places
Price (discounted): currency, 2 decimal places
VAT: currency, 2 decimal places
Penalty: currency, 2 decimal places
Total price: currency, 2 decimal places

Constant input data (area B):
Standard price: currency, 2 decimal places
VAT: numeric, 2 decimal places
Discount: numeric, 2 decimal places
Penalty: currency, 2 decimal places

	A	B	C	D	E	F	G	H	I	J	K
1	Corrib Airlines	Flights from Galway and Sligo									
2	Standard price										
3	VAT rate	Input area B									
4	Discount										
5	Penalty										
6											
7											
8	Seat no.	Name	Age	Luggage	Price	Discount	Price (dis.)	VAT	Penalty	Total price	
9											
10											
11											
12											
13											
14											
15		Input area A					Output area C				
16											
17											
18											
19											
20											
21											
22											
23											

3. *Data-processing formulas:*

E10: **B2**. This must be copied down the column, using an absolute cell reference, as everybody has the same basic price before other considerations.

F10:   **IF C10<12   E10*B4   0**
      (condition)   (true)   (false)

All parts of this formula will be copied down the column, except for B4, which should remain absolute.

G10: **E10–F10**. This will be copied down the column, using relative cell references.

H10: **G10*B3**. G10 will be relative, and B3 will be absolute.

I10:   **IF D10>20   (D10–20)*B5   0**
      (condition)   (true)   (false)

All will have relative cell references, except B5 (the penalty amount, £1), which should be absolute. D10–20 calculates the number of kilograms over the 20 kg limit.

J10:   **G10+H10+I10**. This gives the total price to be charged to each passenger.

4. *Protected data.* Protect all data-processing sections (area C) and headings.

5. *Data entry form.* This is a form that could be used to collect data on paper before entering data, if necessary. Its purpose is to make the entry of data more efficient and to minimise errors. The form does this by

—having items of data to be input in the same order as the spreadsheet
—having a clear heading
—giving format of dates, text, and numbers.

DATA ENTRY FORM
Airline booking system

Name	Age	Luggage weight (kg)
....	....	....
....	....	....
....	....	....
....	....	....
....	....	....
....	....	....
....	....	....
....	....	....
....	....	....
....	....	....
....	....	....

6. *Test data.*

(Note that the test data has a wide range of situations, including true and false responses to discount and penalty charges.)

Corrib Airlines	Flights from Galway and Sligo
Standard price	£50
VAT rate	21%
Discount rate	1%
Penalty	£1

Seat no.	Name	Age	Luggage
1	B. Bradley	45	17
2	C. Collins	5	7
3	D. Collins	11	9
4	M. Collins	26	23
5	A. Doyle	42	18
6	K. Geraghty	7	14
7	P. Hillery	35	21
8	B. Laffey	17	16
9	T. Breen	27	10
10	B. Ryan	10	20
11	D. White	24	17
12	S. Smyth	33	4

7. *Expected output (manually calculated).*

Price	Discount price	Discounted	VAT	Penalty	Total price
£50.00	£0.00	£50.00	£10.50	£0.00	£60.50
£50.00	£5.00	£45.00	£9.45	£0.00	£54.45
£50.00	£5.00	£45.00	£9.45	£0.00	£54.45
£50.00	£0.00	£50.00	£10.50	£3.00	£63.50
£50.00	£0.00	£50.00	£10.50	£0.00	£60.50
£50.00	£5.00	£45.00	£9.45	£0.00	£54.45
£50.00	£0.00	£50.00	£10.50	£1.00	£61.50
£50.00	£0.00	£50.00	£10.50	£0.00	£60.50
£50.00	£0.00	£50.00	£10.50	£0.00	£60.50
£50.00	£5.00	£45.00	£9.45	£0.00	£54.45
£50.00	£0.00	£50.00	£10.50	£0.00	£60.50
£50.00	£0.00	£50.00	£10.50	£0.00	£60.50

8. Spreadsheet print-out.

	A	B	C	D	E	F	G	H	I	J	K
1	Corrib Airlines	Flights from Galway and Sligo									
2	Standard price	£50.00									
3	VAT rate	0.21									
4	Discount	0.1									
5	Penalty	£1.00									
6											
7											
8	Seat no.	Name	Age	Luggage	Price	Discount	Price (dis.)	VAT	Penalty	Total price	
9											
10	1	B. Bradley	45	17	£50.00	£0.00	£50.00	£10.50	£0.00	£60.50	
11	2	C. Collins	5	7	£50.00	£5.00	£45.00	£9.45	£0.00	£54.45	
12	3	D. Collins	11	9	£50.00	£5.00	£45.00	£9.45	£0.00	£54.45	
13	4	M. Collins	26	23	£50.00	£0.00	£50.00	£10.50	£3.00	£63.50	
14	5	A. Doyle	42	18	£50.00	£0.00	£50.00	£10.50	£0.00	£60.50	
15	6	K. Geraghty	7	14	£50.00	£5.00	£45.00	£9.45	£0.00	£54.45	
16	7	P. Hillery	35	21	£50.00	£0.00	£50.00	£10.50	£1.00	£61.50	
17	8	B. Laffey	17	16	£50.00	£0.00	£50.00	£10.50	£0.00	£60.50	
18	9	T. Breen	27	10	£50.00	£0.00	£50.00	£10.50	£0.00	£60.50	
19	10	B. Ryan	10	20	£50.00	£5.00	£45.00	£9.45	£0.00	£54.45	
20	11	D. White	24	17	£50.00	£0.00	£50.00	£10.50	£0.00	£60.50	
21	12	S. Smyth	33	4	£50.00	£0.00	£50.00	£10.50	£0.00	£60.50	
22											

9. Print-out of cell contents (Lotus 1-2-3).

Key:

[w...]   Column width; for example: [w12], column width 12 characters
( )   Format; for example: (c2), currency format, two decimal places
'   Label
@   Built-in function is being used
$ In a cell reference indicates an absolute cell reference

A:A1: [w12] 'Corrib Airlines
A:B1: 'Flights from Galway and Sligo
A:A2: [w12] 'Standard price
A:B2: (c2) 50
A:A3: [w12] 'VAT rate
A:B3: 0.21
A:A4: [w12] 'Discount rate
A:B4: 0.1
A:A5: [w12] 'Penalty
A:B5: (c2) 1
A:A8: [w12] 'Seat no.
A:B8: 'Name
A:C8: Age
A:D8: 'Luggage
A:E8: 'Price
A:F8: 'Discount
A:G8: 'Price (dis.)
A:H8: 'VAT
A:I8: 'Penalty

A:J8: 'Total price
A:A10: [w12] 1
A:B10: 'B. Bradley
A:C10: 45
A:D10: 17
A:E10: (c2) +$B$2
A:F10: (c2) @IF(C10<12,E10*$B$4,0)
A:G10: (c2) +E10–F10
A:H10: (c2) +G10*$B$3
A:I10: (c2) @IF(D10>20,(D10–20)*$B$5,0)
A:J10: (c2) +G10+H10+I10
A:A11: [w12] 2
A:B11: 'C. Collins
A:C11: 5
A:D11: 7
A:E11: (c2) +$B$2
A:F11: (c2) @IF(C11<12,E11*$B$4,0)
A:G11: (c2) +E11–F11
A:H11: (c2) +G11*$B$3
A:I11: (c2) @IF(D11>20,(D11–20)*$B$5,0)
A:J11: (c2) +G11+H11+I11
A:A12: [w12] 3
A:B12: 'D. Collins
A:C12: 11
A:D12: 9
A:E12: (c2) +$B$2
A:F12: (c2) @IF(C12<12,E12*$B$4,0)
A:G12: (c2) +E12–F12
A:H12: (c2) +G12*$B$3
A:I12: (c2) @IF(D12>20,(D12–20)*$B$5,0)
A:J12: (c2) +G12+H12+I12
A:A13: [w12] 4
A:B13: 'M. Collins
A:C13: 26
A:D13: 23
A:E13: (c2) +$B$2
A:F13: (c2) @IF(C13<12,E13*$B$4,0)
A:G13: (c2) +E13–F13
A:H13: (c2) +G13*$B$3
A:I13: (c2) @IF(D13>20,(D13–20)*$B$5,0)
A:J13: (c2) +G13+H13+I13
A:A14: [w12] 5
A:B14: 'A. Doyle

A:C14: 42
A:D14: 18
A:E14: (c2) +$B$2
A:F14: (c2) @IF(C14<12,E14*$B$4,0)
A:G14: (c2) +E14–F14
A:H14: (c2) +G14*$B$3
A:I14: (c2) @IF(D14>20,(D14–20)*$B$5,0)
A:J14: (c2) +G14+H14+I14
A:A15: [w12] 6
A:B15: 'K. Geraghty
A:C15: 7
A:D15: 14
A:E15: (c2) +$B$2
A:F15: (c2) @IF(C15<12,E15*$B$4,0)
A:G15: (c2) +E15–F15
A:H15: (c2) +G15*$B$3
A:I15: (c2) @IF(D15>20,(D15–20)*$B$5,0)
A:J15: (c2) +G15+H15+I15
A:A16: [w12] 7
A:B16: 'P. Hillery
A:C16: 35
A:D16: 21
A:E16: (c2) +$B$2
A:F16: (c2) @IF(C16<12,E16*$B$4,0)
A:G16: (c2) +E16–F16
A:H16: (c2) +G16*$B$3
A:I16: (c2) @IF(D16>20,(D16–20)*$B$5,0)
A:J16: (c2) +G16+H16+I16
A:A17: [w12] 8
A:B17: 'B. Laffey
A:C17: 17
A:D17: 16
A:E17: (c2) +$B$2
A:F17: (c2) @IF(C17<12,E17*$B$4,0)
A:G17: (c2) +E17–F17
A:H17: (c2) +G17*$B$3
A:I17: (c2) @IF(D17>20,(D17–20)*$B$5,0)
A:J17: (c2) +G17+H17+I17
A:A18: [w12] 9

A:B18: 'T. Breen
A:C18: 27
A:D18: 10
A:E18: (c2) +$B$2
A:F18: (c2) @IF(C18<12,E18*$B$4,0)
A:G18: (c2) +E18–F18
A:H18: (c2) +G18*$B$3
A:I18: (c2) @IF(D18>20,(D18–20)*$B$5,0)
A:J18: (c2) +G18+H18+I18
A:A19: [w12] 10
A:B19: 'B. Ryan
A:C19: 10
A:D19: 20
A:E19: (c2) +$B$2
A:F19: (c2) @IF(C19<12,E19*$B$4,0)
A:G19: (c2) +E19–F19
A:H19: (c2) +G19*$B$3
A:I19: (c2) @IF(D19>20,(D19–20)*$B$5,0)
A:J19: (c2) +G19+H19+I19
A:A20: [w12] 11
A:B20: 'D. White
A:C20: 24
A:D20: 17
A:E20: (c2) +$B$2
A:F20: (c2) @IF(C20<12,E20*$B$4,0)
A:G20: (c2) +E20–F20
A:H20: (c2) +G20*$B$3
A:I20: (c2) @IF(D20>20,(D20–20)*$B$5,0)
A:J20: (c2) +G20+H20+I20
A:A21: [w12] 12
A:B21: 'S. Smyth
A:C21: 33
A:D21: 4
A:E21: (c2) +$B$2
A:F21: (c2) @IF(C21<12,E21*$B$4,0)
A:G21: (c2) +E21–F21
A:H21: (c2) +G21*$B$3
A:I21: (c2) @IF(D21>20,(D21–20)*$B$5,0)
A:J21: (c2) +G21+H21+I21

10. *User instructions.* (These are an example only: this set of instructions will vary from system to system.)

(a) How to access the program:
- Switch on the computer
- Wait for the C prompt (C:\>)
- Type **cd lotus123** and press **[enter]**
- Type **lotus** and press **[enter]**
- Wait for Lotus 1-2-3 to load

(b) How to access the file:
- Use the command **/file retrieve airport**
- The spreadsheet will now appear

(c) Entering data:
- Use data entry forms or input data directly.
- Start by entering the data in cells B2 to B5.
- Do not place the pound sign in front of money amounts.
- Enter VAT and discount rates as decimals; for example, 21% is entered as **0.21**.
- Enter seat number, name, age and luggage weight for each passenger.

(d) All other columns are protected and are displayed automatically.

(e) How to save the file:
Use the command **/file save airport1** for the first flight, **airport2** for the second, and so on.

(f) Printing:

To print, use the command **/print printer range A1..J21 [enter] go**.

Personal tax calculations for the year

This spreadsheet example produces the figures required by the Revenue Commissioners for personal tax purposes. The calculation is cumulative, i.e. the tax is charged at a fixed percentage rate on the cumulative taxable pay.

The only inputs to the spreadsheet are

—the standard rates for tax, superannuation, PRSI (employee and total contribution);
—the weekly tax-free allowance.

And for each week:

—the gross pay less superannuation.

All other figures are calculated automatically.

CREATING THE SPREADSHEET

Make sure that standard rates are all formatted as percentages.

Week numbers are quickly produced using a ***counting formula***. The number **1** is entered into cell A11 and the formula **+A11+1** or **=A11+1** is entered in cell A12. This can then be copied down the column for fifty-two weeks.

All money amounts should be in currency format, with two decimal places.

FORMULA EXPLANATIONS

C11 **+B11** brings the payment amount across for the first week. The cumulative amount and the pay will always be the same in the first week.

C12 **C11+B12** cumulates the pay amount and is copied down the cell using relative cell references. It adds the previous cumulative amount (C11) to the present pay amount (B12).

D11 **G6*A11** is the tax-free allowance (TFA) multiplied by the week number. The cumulative TFA is always the weekly TFA by the week number. Note that the weekly amount will remain the same for each week (absolute cell references, usually indicated by use of the $ sign).

E11   **IF C11−D11<0**   **0**   **C121−D11**
    (condition)   (true)   (false)
If the cumulative tax-free allowance is greater than the cumulative pay, then C11−D11 will be less than 0, and therefore the employee should pay no tax (0); otherwise the taxable pay will be the difference between the cumulative pay and the cumulative tax-free allowance.

F11 **E11*D6** works out the cumulative tax, which is calculated by multiplying the rate (D6, which will be an absolute cell reference) by the cumulative taxable pay (E11, which will be relative).

G11 **F11**. In the first week the tax deducted will always be equal to the cumulative tax.

G12   **IF F12<F11**   **0**   **F12−F11**
    (condition)   (true)   (false)
If the cumulative tax this week (total tax due to date) is less than last week, then pay no tax and receive a refund; otherwise pay the difference between this week and last. All cell references will be relative.

H11 **0**. The tax refund will always be nil in the first week.

H12   **IF F12>F11**   **0**   **F11−F12**
    (condition)   (true)   (false)
If the cumulative tax this week (total tax due to date) is greater than last week, then pay no refund; otherwise pay the difference between last week and this week. All cell references will be relative.

I11 **B11*F6** calculates the PRSI contribution of the employee. B11 will be relative and F6 will be absolute.

K11   **IF B11='Uncert.'**   **0**   **1**
    (condition)   (true)   (false)
If a person is on uncertified leave they will not receive credit for insurance purposes in that week (0); otherwise they will get credit (1).

==
TAX DEDUCTION CARD   Employee: Gerard Morgan
==

Rates	Superann.		Tax rate	Emp. share	Total con.	Weekly TFA					
	5.00%		32.00%	7.75%	19.95%	£110.50					

Week no.	Gross less superann.	Cum. gross pay	Cum. TFA	Cum. taxable pay	Cum. tax	Tax deducted	Tax refund	Emp. share	Total contrib.	Insurable week
1	£200.34	£200.34	£110.50	£89.84	£28.75	£28.75	£0.00	£15.53	£39.97	1
2	£200.34	£400.68	£221.00	£179.68	£57.50	£28.75	£0.00	£15.53	£39.97	1
3	£184.77	£585.45	£331.50	£253.95	£81.26	£23.77	£0.00	£14.32	£36.86	1
4	£73.91	£659.36	£442.00	£217.36	£69.56	£0.00	£11.71	£5.73	£14.75	1
5	Uncert.	£659.36	£552.50	£106.86	£34.20	£0.00	£35.36	£0.00	£0.00	1
6	Uncert.	£659.36	£663.00	£0.00	£0.00	£0.00	£34.20	£0.00	£0.00	1
7	£73.91	£733.27	£773.50	£0.00	£0.00	£0.00	£0.00	£5.73	£14.75	1
8	£248.96	£982.23	£884.00	£98.23	£31.43	£31.43	£0.00	£19.29	£49.67	1
9	£195.47	£1,177.70	£994.50	£183.20	£58.62	£27.19	£0.00	£15.15	£39.00	1
10	Uncert.	£1,177.70	£1,105.00	£72.70	£23.26	£0.00	£35.36	£0.00	£0.00	1
11	£200.34	£1,378.04	£1,215.50	£162.54	£52.01	£28.75	£0.00	£15.53	£39.97	1
12	£200.34	£1,578.38	£1,326.00	£252.38	£80.76	£28.75	£0.00	£15.53	£39.97	1
13	£200.34	£1,778.72	£1,436.50	£342.22	£109.51	£28.75	£0.00	£15.53	£39.97	1
14	£200.34	£1,979.06	£1,547.00	£432.06	£138.26	£28.75	£0.00	£15.53	£39.97	1
15	£200.34	£2,179.40	£1,657.50	£521.90	£167.01	£28.75	£0.00	£15.53	£39.97	1
16	£200.34	£2,379.74	£1,768.00	£611.74	£195.76	£28.75	£0.00	£15.53	£39.97	1
17	£643.80	£3,023.54	£1,878.50	£1,145.04	£366.41	£170.66	£0.00	£49.89	£128.44	1
18	H	£3,023.54	£1,989.00	£1,034.54	£331.05	£0.00	£35.36	£0.00	£0.00	1
19	H	£3,023.54	£2,099.50	£924.04	£295.69	£0.00	£35.36	£0.00	£0.00	1
20	H	£3,023.54	£2,210.00	£813.54	£260.33	£0.00	£35.36	£0.00	£0.00	1
21	£200.34	£3,223.88	£2,320.50	£903.38	£289.08	£28.75	£0.00	£15.53	£39.97	1
22	£200.34	£3,424.22	£2,431.00	£993.22	£317.83	£28.75	£0.00	£15.53	£39.97	1
23	£200.34	£3,624.56	£2,541.50	£1,083.06	£346.58	£28.75	£0.00	£15.53	£39.97	1
24	£200.34	£3,824.90	£2,652.00	£1,172.90	£375.33	£28.75	£0.00	£15.53	£39.97	1
25	£200.34	£4,025.24	£2,762.50	£1,262.74	£404.08	£28.75	£0.00	£15.53	£39.97	1
26	£200.34	£4,225.58	£2,873.00	£1,352.58	£432.83	£28.75	£0.00	£15.53	£39.97	1
27	£200.34	£4,425.92	£2,983.50	£1,442.42	£461.57	£28.75	£0.00	£15.53	£39.97	1
28	£200.34	£4,626.26	£3,094.00	£1,532.26	£490.32	£28.75	£0.00	£15.53	£39.97	1
29	£195.47	£4,822.23	£3,204.50	£1,617.73	£517.67	£27.35	£0.00	£15.19	£39.10	1
30	£200.34	£5,022.57	£3,315.00	£1,707.57	£546.42	£28.75	£0.00	£15.53	£39.97	1
31	£200.34	£5,222.91	£3,425.50	£1,797.41	£575.17	£28.75	£0.00	£15.53	£39.97	1
32	£200.34	£5,423.25	£3,536.00	£1,887.25	£603.92	£28.75	£0.00	£15.53	£39.97	1
33	£200.34	£5,623.59	£3,646.50	£1,977.09	£632.67	£28.75	£0.00	£15.53	£39.97	1
34	£200.34	£5,823.93	£3,757.00	£2,066.93	£661.42	£28.75	£0.00	£15.53	£39.97	1
35	£200.34	£6,024.27	£3,867.50	£2,156.77	£690.17	£28.75	£0.00	£15.53	£39.97	1
36	£200.34	£6,224.61	£3,978.00	£2,246.61	£718.92	£28.75	£0.00	£15.53	£39.97	1
37	£348.16	£6,572.77	£4,088.50	£2,484.27	£794.97	£76.05	£0.00	£26.98	£69.46	1
38	H	£6,572.77	£4,199.00	£2,373.77	£759.61	£0.00	£35.36	£0.00	£0.00	1
39	£195.47	£6,768.24	£4,309.50	£2,458.74	£786.80	£27.19	£0.00	£15.15	£39.00	1
40	£200.34	£6,968.58	£4,420.00	£2,548.58	£815.55	£28.75	£0.00	£15.53	£39.97	1
41	£200.34	£7,168.92	£4,530.50	£2,638.42	£844.29	£28.75	£0.00	£15.53	£39.97	1
42	£200.34	£7,369.26	£4,641.00	£2,728.26	£873.04	£28.75	£0.00	£15.53	£39.97	1
43	£200.34	£7,569.60	£4,751.50	£2,818.10	£901.79	£28.75	£0.00	£15.53	£39.97	1
44	£200.34	£7,769.94	£4,862.00	£2,907.94	£930.54	£28.75	£0.00	£15.53	£39.97	1
45	£200.34	£7,970.28	£4,972.50	£2,997.78	£959.29	£28.75	£0.00	£15.53	£39.97	1
46	£200.34	£8,170.62	£5,083.00	£3,087.62	£988.04	£28.75	£0.00	£15.53	£39.97	1
47	£200.34	£8,370.96	£5,193.50	£3,177.46	£1,016.79	£28.75	£0.00	£15.53	£39.97	1
48	£195.47	£8,566.43	£5,304.00	£3,262.43	£1,043.98	£27.19	£0.00	£15.15	£39.00	1
49	£200.34	£8,766.77	£5,414.50	£3,352.27	£1,072.73	£28.75	£0.00	£15.53	£39.97	1
50	£200.34	£8,967.11	£5,525.00	£3,442.11	£1,101.48	£28.75	£0.00	£15.53	£39.97	1
51	£200.34	£9,167.45	£5,635.50	£3,531.95	£1,130.22	£28.75	£0.00	£15.53	£39.97	1
52	£195.47	£9,362.92	£5,746.00	£3,616.92	£1,157.41	£27.19	£0.00	£15.15	£39.00	1

Total insurable weeks: 49

40

	A	B	C	D	E	F	G	H	I	J	K
1		TAX DEDU									
2											
3											
4											
5	Rates	Super ann.		Tax rate	Emp. share	Total con.					
6		0.05		0.32	0.0775	0.1995					
7											
8	week no.	Gross less	Cum. gross	Cum.	Cum.	weekly TFA		Emp.	Total	Insurable	
9		superann.	pay	TFA	taxable pay			share	contrib.	week	
10						110.5					
11	1	200.34	=B11	=$G$6*A11	=C11-D11	=E11	0	=B11*$E$6	=B11*$F$6	=IF(B11>=Uncert.,0,1)	
12	=A11+1	200.34	=C11+B12	=$G$6*A12	=C12-D12	=E11*$G$6	=IF(F12>F11,0,F11-F12)	=B12*$E$6	=B12*$F$6	=IF(B12>=Uncert.,0,1)	
13	=A12+1	184.77	=C12+B13	=$G$6*A13	=C13-D13	=E11*$G$6	=IF(F13>F12,0,F12-F13)	=B13*$E$6	=B13*$F$6	=IF(B13>=Uncert.,0,1)	
14	=A13+1	73.91	=C13+B14	=$G$6*A14	=C14-D14	=E11*$G$6	=IF(F14>F13,0,F13-F14)	=B14*$E$6	=B14*$F$6	=IF(B14>=Uncert.,0,1)	
15	=A14+1	Uncert.	=C14+B15	=$G$6*A15	=C15-D15	=E11*$G$6	=IF(F15>F14,0,F14-F15)	=B15*$E$6	=B15*$F$6	=IF(B15>=Uncert.,0,1)	
16	=A15+1	Uncert.	=C15+B16	=$G$6*A16	=C16-D16	=E11*$G$6	=IF(F16>F15,0,F15-F16)	=B16*$E$6	=B16*$F$6	=IF(B16>=Uncert.,0,1)	
17	=A16+1	73.91	=C16+B17	=$G$6*A17	=C17-D17	=E11*$G$6	=IF(F17>F16,0,F16-F17)	=B17*$E$6	=B17*$F$6	=IF(B17>=Uncert.,0,1)	
18	=A17+1	248.96	=C17+B18	=$G$6*A18	=C18-D18	=E11*$G$6	=IF(F18>F17,0,F17-F18)	=B18*$E$6	=B18*$F$6	=IF(B18>=Uncert.,0,1)	
19	=A18+1	195.47	=C18+B19	=$G$6*A19	=C19-D19	=E11*$G$6	=IF(F19>F18,0,F18-F19)	=B19*$E$6	=B19*$F$6	=IF(B19>=Uncert.,0,1)	
20	=A19+1	Uncert.	=C19+B20	=$G$6*A20	=C20-D20	=E11*$G$6	=IF(F20>F19,0,F19-F20)	=B20*$E$6	=B20*$F$6	=IF(B20>=Uncert.,0,1)	
21	=A20+1	200.34	=C20+B21	=$G$6*A21	=C21-D21	=E11*$G$6	=IF(F21>F20,0,F20-F21)	=B21*$E$6	=B21*$F$6	=IF(B21>=Uncert.,0,1)	
22	=A21+1	200.34	=C21+B22	=$G$6*A22	=C22-D22	=E11*$G$6	=IF(F22>F21,0,F21-F22)	=B22*$E$6	=B22*$F$6	=IF(B22>=Uncert.,0,1)	
23	=A22+1	200.34	=C22+B23	=$G$6*A23	=C23-D23	=E11*$G$6	=IF(F23>F22,0,F22-F23)	=B23*$E$6	=B23*$F$6	=IF(B23>=Uncert.,0,1)	
24	=A23+1	200.34	=C23+B24	=$G$6*A24	=C24-D24	=E11*$G$6	=IF(F24>F23,0,F23-F24)	=B24*$E$6	=B24*$F$6	=IF(B24>=Uncert.,0,1)	
25	=A24+1	200.34	=C24+B25	=$G$6*A25	=C25-D25	=E11*$G$6	=IF(F25>F24,0,F24-F25)	=B25*$E$6	=B25*$F$6	=IF(B25>=Uncert.,0,1)	
26	=A25+1	200.34	=C25+B26	=$G$6*A26	=C26-D26	=E11*$G$6	=IF(F26>F25,0,F25-F26)	=B26*$E$6	=B26*$F$6	=IF(B26>=Uncert.,0,1)	
27	=A26+1	643.8	=C26+B27	=$G$6*A27	=C27-D27	=E11*$G$6	=IF(F27>F26,0,F26-F27)	=B27*$E$6	=B27*$F$6	=IF(B27>=Uncert.,0,1)	
28	=A27+1	H	=C27+B28	=$G$6*A28	=C28-D28	=E11*$G$6	=IF(F28>F27,0,F27-F28)	=B28*$E$6	=B28*$F$6	=IF(B28>=Uncert.,0,1)	
29	=A28+1	H	=C28+B29	=$G$6*A29	=C29-D29	=E11*$G$6	=IF(F29>F28,0,F28-F29)	=B29*$E$6	=B29*$F$6	=IF(B29>=Uncert.,0,1)	
30	=A29+1	H	=C29+B30	=$G$6*A30	=C30-D30	=E11*$G$6	=IF(F30>F29,0,F29-F30)	=B30*$E$6	=B30*$F$6	=IF(B30>=Uncert.,0,1)	
31	=A30+1	200.34	=C30+B31	=$G$6*A31	=C31-D31	=E11*$G$6	=IF(F31>F30,0,F30-F31)	=B31*$E$6	=B31*$F$6	=IF(B31>=Uncert.,0,1)	
32	=A31+1	200.34	=C31+B32	=$G$6*A32	=C32-D32	=E11*$G$6	=IF(F32>F31,0,F31-F32)	=B32*$E$6	=B32*$F$6	=IF(B32>=Uncert.,0,1)	
33	=A32+1	200.34	=C32+B33	=$G$6*A33	=C33-D33	=E11*$G$6	=IF(F33>F32,0,F32-F33)	=B33*$E$6	=B33*$F$6	=IF(B33>=Uncert.,0,1)	
34	=A33+1	200.34	=C33+B34	=$G$6*A34	=C34-D34	=E11*$G$6	=IF(F34>F33,0,F33-F34)	=B34*$E$6	=B34*$F$6	=IF(B34>=Uncert.,0,1)	
35	=A34+1	200.34	=C34+B35	=$G$6*A35	=C35-D35	=E11*$G$6	=IF(F35>F34,0,F34-F35)	=B35*$E$6	=B35*$F$6	=IF(B35>=Uncert.,0,1)	
36	=A35+1	200.34	=C35+B36	=$G$6*A36	=C36-D36	=E11*$G$6	=IF(F36>F35,0,F35-F36)	=B36*$E$6	=B36*$F$6	=IF(B36>=Uncert.,0,1)	
37	=A36+1	200.34	=C36+B37	=$G$6*A37	=C37-D37	=E11*$G$6	=IF(F37>F36,0,F36-F37)	=B37*$E$6	=B37*$F$6	=IF(B37>=Uncert.,0,1)	
38	=A37+1	195.97	=C37+B38	=$G$6*A38	=C38-D38	=E11*$G$6	=IF(F38>F37,0,F37-F38)	=B38*$E$6	=B38*$F$6	=IF(B38>=Uncert.,0,1)	
39	=A38+1	200.34	=C38+B39	=$G$6*A39	=C39-D39	=E11*$G$6	=IF(F39>F38,0,F38-F39)	=B39*$E$6	=B39*$F$6	=IF(B39>=Uncert.,0,1)	
40	=A39+1	200.34	=C39+B40	=$G$6*A40	=C40-D40	=E11*$G$6	=IF(F40>F39,0,F39-F40)	=B40*$E$6	=B40*$F$6	=IF(B40>=Uncert.,0,1)	
41	=A40+1	200.34	=C40+B41	=$G$6*A41	=C41-D41	=E11*$G$6	=IF(F41>F40,0,F40-F41)	=B41*$E$6	=B41*$F$6	=IF(B41>=Uncert.,0,1)	
42	=A41+1	200.34	=C41+B42	=$G$6*A42	=C42-D42	=E11*$G$6	=IF(F42>F41,0,F41-F42)	=B42*$E$6	=B42*$F$6	=IF(B42>=Uncert.,0,1)	
43	=A42+1	200.34	=C42+B43	=$G$6*A43	=C43-D43	=E11*$G$6	=IF(F43>F42,0,F42-F43)	=B43*$E$6	=B43*$F$6	=IF(B43>=Uncert.,0,1)	
44	=A43+1	200.34	=C43+B44	=$G$6*A44	=C44-D44	=E11*$G$6	=IF(F44>F43,0,F43-F44)	=B44*$E$6	=B44*$F$6	=IF(B44>=Uncert.,0,1)	
45	=A44+1	200.34	=C44+B45	=$G$6*A45	=C45-D45	=E11*$G$6	=IF(F45>F44,0,F44-F45)	=B45*$E$6	=B45*$F$6	=IF(B45>=Uncert.,0,1)	
46	=A45+1	200.34	=C45+B46	=$G$6*A46	=C46-D46	=E11*$G$6	=IF(F46>F45,0,F45-F46)	=B46*$E$6	=B46*$F$6	=IF(B46>=Uncert.,0,1)	
47	=A46+1	348.16	=C46+B47	=$G$6*A47	=C47-D47	=E11*$G$6	=IF(F47>F46,0,F46-F47)	=B47*$E$6	=B47*$F$6	=IF(B47>=Uncert.,0,1)	
48	=A47+1	H	=C47+B48	=$G$6*A48	=C48-D48	=E11*$G$6	=IF(F48>F47,0,F47-F48)	=B48*$E$6	=B48*$F$6	=IF(B48>=Uncert.,0,1)	
49	=A48+1	195.47	=C48+B49	=$G$6*A49	=C49-D49	=E11*$G$6	=IF(F49>F48,0,F48-F49)	=B49*$E$6	=B49*$F$6	=IF(B49>=Uncert.,0,1)	
50	=A49+1	200.34	=C49+B50	=$G$6*A50	=C50-D50	=E11*$G$6	=IF(F50>F49,0,F49-F50)	=B50*$E$6	=B50*$F$6	=IF(B50>=Uncert.,0,1)	
51	=A50+1	200.34	=C50+B51	=$G$6*A51	=C51-D51	=E11*$G$6	=IF(F51>F50,0,F50-F51)	=B51*$E$6	=B51*$F$6	=IF(B51>=Uncert.,0,1)	
52	=A51+1	200.34	=C51+B52	=$G$6*A52	=C52-D52	=E11*$G$6	=IF(F52>F51,0,F51-F52)	=B52*$E$6	=B52*$F$6	=IF(B52>=Uncert.,0,1)	
53	=A52+1	200.34	=C52+B53	=$G$6*A53	=C53-D53	=E11*$G$6	=IF(F53>F52,0,F52-F53)	=B53*$E$6	=B53*$F$6	=IF(B53>=Uncert.,0,1)	
54	=A53+1	200.34	=C53+B54	=$G$6*A54	=C54-D54	=E11*$G$6	=IF(F54>F53,0,F53-F54)	=B54*$E$6	=B54*$F$6	=IF(B54>=Uncert.,0,1)	
55	=A54+1	200.34	=C54+B55	=$G$6*A55	=C55-D55	=E11*$G$6	=IF(F55>F54,0,F54-F55)	=B55*$E$6	=B55*$F$6	=IF(B55>=Uncert.,0,1)	
56	=A55+1	200.34	=C55+B56	=$G$6*A56	=C56-D56	=E11*$G$6	=IF(F56>F55,0,F55-F56)	=B56*$E$6	=B56*$F$6	=IF(B56>=Uncert.,0,1)	
57	=A56+1	200.34	=C56+B57	=$G$6*A57	=C57-D57	=E11*$G$6	=IF(F57>F56,0,F56-F57)	=B57*$E$6	=B57*$F$6	=IF(B57>=Uncert.,0,1)	
58	=A57+1	195.47	=C57+B58	=$G$6*A58	=C58-D58	=E11*$G$6	=IF(F58>F57,0,F57-F58)	=B58*$E$6	=B58*$F$6	=IF(B58>=Uncert.,0,1)	
59	=A58+1	200.34	=C58+B59	=$G$6*A59	=C59-D59	=E11*$G$6	=IF(F59>F58,0,F58-F59)	=B59*$E$6	=B59*$F$6	=IF(B59>=Uncert.,0,1)	
60	=A59+1	200.34	=C59+B60	=$G$6*A60	=C60-D60	=E11*$G$6	=IF(F60>F59,0,F59-F60)	=B60*$E$6	=B60*$F$6	=IF(B60>=Uncert.,0,1)	
61	=A60+1	200.34	=C60+B61	=$G$6*A61	=C61-D61	=E11*$G$6	=IF(F61>F60,0,F60-F61)	=B61*$E$6	=B61*$F$6	=IF(B61>=Uncert.,0,1)	
62	=A61+1	195.47	=C61+B62	=$G$6*A62	=C62-D62	=E11*$G$6	=IF(F62>F61,0,F61-F62)	=B62*$E$6	=B62*$F$6	=IF(B62>=Uncert.,0,1)	
63								Total Insurab		=SUM(K11:K62)	
64											

Spreadsheet assignments—intermediate level

FUNCTIONS AND COMMANDS REQUIRED FOR ASSIGNMENTS

These assignments are graded, and you are advised to work through them in the order in which they are presented.

As you progress through the assignments you will discover that in order to carry out an assignment you will need to know the functions and commands specific to your spreadsheet program. You will also be practising commands and functions learnt in earlier assignments. The specific commands required for each assignment are given below. (It is assumed that you have covered all the commands required in section 1.)

Some assignments require that you have some background knowledge of the problem involved in the question. This is indicated under the heading 'Concept understanding'.

ASSIGNMENT 1

Concept understanding: area

—Design and documentation of a spreadsheet

—Formula manipulation

—Rounding numbers

—Using the 'if' function

ASSIGNMENT 2

Concept understanding: simple and compound interest

—Formula for accumulating numbers

—Absolute and relative cell reference replication

—Performing 'what if?' calculations

—Line graph with two lines

—Printing the spreadsheet

ASSIGNMENT 3

Concept understanding: declining balance depreciation

As assignment 2 and

—Complex formula manipulation

ASSIGNMENT 4

Concept understanding: break-even point, fixed costs, variable costs, total costs, mark-up

—Line graph and printing

—The 'if' function

ASSIGNMENT 5

Concept understanding: solving quadratic equations

ASSIGNMENT 6
—Maximum, minimum, average functions
—Bar graphs, line graphs

ASSIGNMENT 1

A painter provides an estimate (produced manually) of the cost of painting a room. He has now purchased a computer and has a spreadsheet program. He is keen to have this procedure computerised to allow the production of an estimate of the cost of painting any room.

The manual calculation involves knowing the following details to estimate the cost of painting any room:

—Room dimensions (in metres): height, width, length
—Colour required (four choices only): magnolia, white, light blue, peach
—Exclusions (areas not painted): height, width
—Door and window dimensions

The following information is also available regarding paint coverage and costs:

	Magnolia	White	Light blue	Peach
Cost per litre	£4.00	£3.00	£3.50	£3.50
Coverage per litre	$4 m^2$	$4 m^2$	$2.7 m^2$	$2.95 m^2$

Material costs
Brush   £2.00
Roller   £2.33

The quantity of equipment required is based on the total area to be painted:

Number of brushes: 1 per 50 m
Number of rollers: 1 per 60 m

The number of brushes or rollers to be used is always rounded to the nearest whole number.

The labour charge is based on the area to be painted. This painter charges £1.50 per square metre.

The estimate shows the following information:

- The total area of the walls to be painted (2 × height × length) + (2 × height × width) (A)
- The total area of the exclusions (B)
- The actual area to be painted ($A - B$)
- The cost of paint for the room, taking into account the coverage and cost of the paint:

  Cost of paint = (actual area to be painted ÷ coverage) × cost of paint per litre

- The labour charge:
  Labour charge = actual area to be painted × rate per square metre
- The total materials cost
- The total charge
- Discount, calculated as follows: if the total charge is greater than £50 the discount is 3%; otherwise there is no discount

- VAT, to be charged at 21% on the total charge minus discount
- The total charge payable by the customer

The above information should be produced in the following format, including a full breakdown of the charges:

Jimmy Murphy
14 Fox's Lane
Jobstown, Co. Dublin
Telephone (01) 4535633
Fax (01) 4535561

Customer estimate

Customer name: ....
Address: ....
....
....

Colour required: ....
Total area of room: .... m²
Less exclusions: .... m²
Actual area to be painted: .... m²

Materials costs:	Magnolia	White	Light blue	Peach	Totals
Paint:	....	....	....	....	....

Number of brushes: .... @ £......... ....
Number of rollers: .... @ £......... ....
Labour charge: .... @ £.........   ....
Less discount: ....
Add VAT: ....
Total charge: ....

1. Design a spreadsheet on paper to provide this information to the painter. It should have the minimum number of inputs to produce the final estimate. Use the design and documentation guidelines given in this section.
2. Set up the designed spreadsheet on a computer and use it to calculate the cost of painting the following room:

	Height	Width	Length
Dimensions	3 m	5 m	8 m
Door (1)	2 m	1 m	
Window (1)	3 m	1.5 m	

The colour required is peach.
Save this as ROOM1, and make a print-out of the customer estimate only.

3. Use your spreadsheet again to calculate the cost of painting the following room:

	Height	Width	Length
Dimensions	3 m	6.2 m	12 m
Door	2 m	1 m	
Window	2.5 m	5 m	

The colour required is magnolia.

Save this as ROOM2, and make a print-out of the customer invoice only.

4. Document this spreadsheet completely.

ASSIGNMENT 2

An investment manager requires a spreadsheet to calculate simple and compound interest on different starting investments (principal) over a number of years.

Interest for one year is found by using the formula

$$\text{Interest} = P \times R \div 100$$

where P is the principal and R is the rate.

Remember that with simple interest the principal is the same every year, and therefore the interest is also the same. Compound interest is worked on a different principal each year, which includes the interest of the previous years; for example:

Find the compound interest and simple interest on £100 for two years at 8%.

	Simple	Compound
Year 1	(100 × 8) ÷ 100 = 8	(100 × 8) ÷ 100 = 8
Year 2	(100 × 8) ÷ 100 = 8	(108 × 8) ÷ 100 = 8.64
Totals (interest)	£16	£16.64

1. Set up the spreadsheet as given below, which shows the simple interest and principal for twenty years, using the appropriate formulas and relative and absolute replication. Make sure that all money amounts are in cash format.

    The only inputs in your spreadsheet are the year, principal, and interest rate: all other figures should be calculated automatically by the program.

    Hint: The 'Total simple interest' column cumulates interest. In the first year it will be the same as the 'simple interest' amount. The formula in D11 will be **+C11**. In the second year it will be the previous total plus the simple interest of the second year. The formula in D12 will be **+D11+C12**. This can then be copied down column D using relative cell references. The same procedure will be used to cumulate other columns of data.

	A	B	C	D	E	F	G	H
1	COMPOUND VERSUS SIMPLE INTEREST							
2								
3	Principal	£150.00						
4	Year	1990						
5	Rate (%)	9						
6								
7								
8		Simple	Simple	Tot. simple	Compound	Compound	Tot. com.	
9	Year	principal	interest	interest	principal	interest	interest	
10								
11	1990	£150.00	£13.50	£13.50	£150.00	£13.50	£13.50	
12	1991	£150.00	£13.50	£27.00	£163.50	£14.72	£28.22	
13	1992	£150.00	£13.50	£40.50	£178.22	£16.04	£44.25	
14	1993	£150.00	£13.50	£54.00	£194.25	£17.48	£61.74	
15	1994	£150.00	£13.50	£67.50	£211.74	£19.06	£80.79	
16	1995	£150.00	£13.50	£81.00	£230.79	£20.77	£101.57	
17	1996	£150.00	£13.50	£94.50	£251.57	£22.64	£124.21	
18	1997	£150.00	£13.50	£108.00	£274.21	£24.68	£148.88	
19	1998	£150.00	£13.50	£121.50	£298.88	£26.90	£175.78	
20	1999	£150.00	£13.50	£135.00	£325.78	£29.32	£205.10	
21	2000	£150.00	£13.50	£148.50	£355.10	£31.96	£237.06	
22	2001	£150.00	£13.50	£162.00	£387.06	£34.84	£271.90	
23	2002	£150.00	£13.50	£175.50	£421.90	£37.97	£309.87	
24	2003	£150.00	£13.50	£189.00	£459.87	£41.39	£351.26	
25	2004	£150.00	£13.50	£202.50	£501.26	£45.11	£396.37	
26	2005	£150.00	£13.50	£216.00	£546.37	£49.17	£445.55	
27								

2. *'What if?' calculations.* Write the answers to these questions on a sheet of paper.
   (a) Using the set-up example, say what the compound and simple interest would be on £300 at 13% invested in 1990 for fifteen years.
   (b) Using the set-up example, say what the compound and simple interest would be on £250 at 11.13% invested in 1990 for fourteen years.
   (c) Which of these two investments gives the greater interest: £1,050 at 12% for five years, compound interest, or £1,200 at 12% for five years, simple interest?
3. Add a new column to your spreadsheet to the right of the 'Tot. com. interest' column to show the difference between simple and compound interest for each year. Use a suitable heading.
4. *'What if?' again.*
   (a) If the difference between simple and compound interest on a sum of money invested for two years at 6% is £36, what is the sum?
   (b) If the difference between simple and compound interest on a sum of money invested for ten years at 9% is £38.50, what is the sum?
5. Produce a line graph showing both total simple interest and total compound interest for each year. (If it is not possible to show both lines on the same graph, produce two separate graphs.)

Remember that the x axis (horizontal axis) will show the different years and the y axis (vertical axis) will show the money amounts. Also, use the same scale on both graphs for comparison purposes.

6. Save the spreadsheet as INTEREST, and print it.

ASSIGNMENT 3

Depreciation is the wear and tear cost to a business on the assets it owns. This cost tends to vary from year to year, depending on the method of depreciation used.

The method used here is the **declining balance**. This is similar to the concept of compound interest, except that it is reducing in value all the time; for example:

Asset: car
Cost: £1,000
Number of years of life: 3
Rate of depreciation: 10%

Year	Depreciation	Cumulative depreciation	Net book value
1	100 (1,000 × 0.1)	100	900 (1,000 − 100)
2	90 (900 × 0.1)	190 (100 + 90)	810 (1,000 − 190)
3	81 (810 × 0.1)	271 (190 + 81)	729 (1,000 − 271)

The accounts manager is keen on introducing a computerised spreadsheet in order to calculate depreciation amounts over several years.

The only inputs by the user should be asset, year, cost, and deprecation rate. All other figures should be worked out automatically.

1. Set up the spreadsheet using the information given below, using appropriate formulas and relative and absolute replication, and save this spreadsheet as DEPREC1.
2. Show the depreciation details for the following asset by recalling DEPREC1 and changing the variable information. No formulas should be changed. Save this new information as DEPREC2.

> Item: Ford Escort van
> Year: 1990
> Cost: £6,000
> Estimated life: 5 years
> Deprecation rate: 23.89%

3. Set up a new column to highlight the year (marked *) when the cumulative depreciation is 80 per cent of the original cost. Use the 'if' function.
4. Add a new input to include scrap value, between the rows containing cost and rate inputs (row 8).
5. Get the program to calculate the rate of deprecation rather than having it as an input, by entering the following formula in the rate cell (B9):

$$(1-(S/C)^{\wedge}(1/n))*100$$

where S is the scrap value, C is the cost, and n is the the number of years of life for the asset. (Remember that ^ means 'to the power of'.)

Using the new automatic rate, show the depreciation details for the following.

>Item: Autoprinter
>Year: 1990
>Estimated life: 8 years
>Cost: £40,000
>Scrap value: £5,000

Note: After the eighth year the scrap value should be equal to the net book value in that year: £5,000.

6. What depreciation charge would be used if the scrap value was to be £679.99 after ten years?

    Note: After the tenth year the scrap value should be equal to the net book value in that year: £679.99.

	A	B	C	D	E
1	DEPRECIATION SCHEDULE				
2					
3	Item	IBM Microcomputer			
4	Year	1989			
5	Years	10			
6	Cost	£1,000			
7					
8	Rate (%)	25			
9	--				
10	Year	Deprec.	Cum.	Net book value	
11	--				
12	1989	£250.00	£250.00	£750.00	
13	1990	£187.50	£437.50	£562.50	
14	1991	£140.63	£578.13	£421.88	
15	1992	£105.47	£683.59	£316.41	
16	1993	£79.10	£762.70	£237.30	
17	1994	£59.33	£822.02	£177.98	
18	1995	£44.49	£866.52	£133.48	
19	1996	£33.37	£899.89	£100.11	
20	1997	£25.03	£924.92	£75.08	
21	1998	£18.77	£943.69	£56.31	
22					

ASSIGNMENT 4

The management need to know at what point in production the firm has 'broken even' or earned sufficient revenue to cover all costs. This point is commonly known as the break-even point. An example would be where a newspaper needs to sell 20,000 copies a day to break even. Any further revenue earned after this point will be a contribution to profit—or, if below break-even, then it is a contribution against losses.

You work in the Accounts Department of Plasta Systems Ltd, a company that produces components for the engineering industry. The cost figures below relate to an estimated production of 10,000 units of product Z23 in the year.

	£ Fixed	£ Variable
Direct labour	125,000	35,000
Direct materials		120,000
Overheads:		
Factory	65,000	15,000
Distribution	48,000	12,000
Advertising	31,000	

1. Design and document a spreadsheet on paper to allow the input of
   —variable and fixed costs;
   —the number of units that the costs are based on (10,000 in this example);
   —the mark-up (the percentage the company adds to the unit cost to calculate a price).
2. The design should output all the following costing information based on the given formulas:

   - Total cost = total fixed costs + total variable costs
   - Cost per unit = total cost ÷ number of units produced
   - Variable cost per unit = total variable cost ÷ number of units produced
   - Selling price = cost per unit + (cost per unit × mark-up percentage)
   - Contribution per unit = selling price ÷ variable cost per unit
   - Break-even units = total fixed cost ÷ contribution per unit
   - Break-even revenue = break-even units × selling price
   - Total profit = number of units produced × contribution per unit – total fixed costs

3. The design should generate a line graph to show the three lines, indicating clearly the break-even point (the intersection point between the total cost line and the total revenue line).

   - Total revenue line: line starts at (0,0)
   - Total cost line: line starts at (0,*total fixed cost*)
   - Total fixed cost line: straight horizontal line

   It may be useful to use a table to produce the graph of each line.

Units	Total cost	Total fixed cost	Total revenue
0	Total fixed cost	Total fixed cost	0
1,000	1,000 × cost per unit	Total fixed cost	1,000 × selling price
2,000	2,000 × cost per unit	Total fixed cost	2,000 × selling price
3,000	etc.		
4,000			
5,000			
6,000			
7,000			
8,000			
9,000			
10,000			

The *x* axis will show the number of units and the *y* axis the money amounts.

4. When the design is complete, set it up on a computer spreadsheet, and use this to answer the following 'what if?' questions:

    (a) The company is considering a new strategy. If it increased its advertising costs to £80,000, research shows that sales would increase to 12,000 units. Would this be a worthwhile strategy? (Compare the old total profit figure based on 10,000 units and advertising of £31,000 with the new total profit figure based on 12,000 units and £80,000 advertising expense.)

    (b) Another strategy is to speed up deliveries, which would increase the distribution expenses to £67,000. Research shows that this strategy should generate 11,650 sales in units. Would this strategy be better than the previous strategy, and why?

    Save this spreadsheet as COSTZ23.

5. The following costs are based on 5,000 units for product Z12:

	Fixed	Variable
Direct labour	12,000	36,000
Direct materials		55,000
Overheads:		
Factory	20,250	2250
Distribution	13,500	
Advertising	17,500	
Mark-up: 25 per cent		

   Enter this information into your spreadsheet and show the costing information and break-even graph. Save this spreadsheet as COSTZ12.

ASSIGNMENT 5

A quadratic equation in x contains terms in x^2 and x and a constant. Two examples are:

$$6x^2 + 12x - 16 = 0$$
$$5x^2 - 3x + 7 = 0$$

However, the x term or the constant may be missing; but if there is an x^2 term the equation is quadratic. Examples are:

$$2x^2 + 4x = 0$$
$$6x^2 - 6 = 0$$

Solving a quadratic equation involves finding which two x values satisfy (solve) it; for example, the equation

$$x^2 - 8x + 15 = 0$$

is satisfied (solved) either by $x = 5$ or by $x = 3$

i.e. $(5 \times 5) - (8 \times 5) + 15 = 25 - 40 + 15 = 0$
or $(3 \times 3) - (8 \times 3) + 15 = 9 - 24 + 15 = 0$

To solve *any* quadratic equation, a formula can be used. For the quadratic equation $ax^2 + bx + c = 0$,

$$x = (-b + (b^2 - 4ac)^{0.5}) \div 2a$$

or

$$x = (-b - (b^2 - 4ac)^{0.5}) \div 2a$$

Example: Solve the following quadratic equation:

$$x^2 + 3x - 11 = 0$$

In this case we have $a = 1$, $b = 3$, and $c = -11$, so

$$x = -3 + ((3)2 - 4(1)(-11))^{0.5} \div 2(1)$$
$$= 2.14$$

or

$$x = -3 - ((3)2 - 4(1)(-11))^{0.5} \div 2(1)$$
$$= -5.14$$

1. Set up a spreadsheet to allow a user to enter any quadratic equation and to output the two solutions. You may use the following headings:

   | x^2 | x | Constant |

   Input

2. If $b^2 < 4ac$ then there is no solution to the quadratic equation. A check should be done on all inputs and an indication given that there is no solution to the equation. (Use the 'if' function.)

3. All solutions should be double-checked. This involves using the solutions in place of x to check that the solution solves the equation (i.e. is equal to 0) by means of the spreadsheet.

4. Solve the following quadratic equations using the set-up spreadsheet:
   - (a) $x^2 + 7x - 2 = 0$
   - (b) $2x^2 + 9x - 7 = 0$
   - (c) $3x^2 - 6x + 2 = 0$
   - (d) $15x^2 + x - 2 = 0$
   - (e) $3x^2 - 8x + 5 = 0$
   - (f) $x^2 - 10x + 25 = 0$
   - (g) $3x^2 - 4x + 2 = 0$

ASSIGNMENT 6

This spreadsheet is used to keep a record of share prices so that the progress of the shares can be analysed and compared. The only inputs are the financial data (which can be imported or keyed in directly). All the other calculations are automatically calculated by the program.

1. Set up the spreadsheet template as given below for storing share price information. Save the template as TEMP.

Stock exchange analysis sheet
Share prices for

Date	AIB	BOI	Jones	CRH	Crean
1/01	3.25	2.00	3.00	1.78	0.89
2/01	3.15	2.10	3.61	1.57	1.22
3/01	3.00	2.10	3.40	1.56	1.34
4/01	2.99	2.10	3.58	1.78	1.78
5/01	3.22	2.58	3.34	1.77	1.56
6/01	3.20	2.58	3.69	1.77	1.76
7/01	3.20	2.57	3.68	1.77	1.45
8/01					
9/01					
10/01					
11/01					
12/01					
13/01					
14/01					
15/01					
16/01					
17/01					
18/01					
19/01					
20/01					
21/01					

Week 1 high
Week 1 low
Week 1 average
Week change

Week 2 high
Week 2 low
Week 2 average
Week change

Week 3 high
Week 3 low
Week 3 average
Week change

Three-week high
Three-week low
Three-week average
Three-week change

2. Set up a separate spreadsheet to store the following information for share prices from 8 January to 14 January:

3.30	2.45	3.91	1.80	1.67
3.30	2.34	3.25	1.80	1.56
3.30	2.67	3.46	1.80	1.56
3.30	2.44	3.35	1.56	1.67
3.32	2.44	3.14	1.47	1.76
3.32	2.45	3.93	1.98	1.32
3.43	2.33	3.55	2.00	1.32

Save this information as WEEK2.

3. Set up a separate spreadsheet to store the following information for share prices from 15 January to 21 January:

3.50	2.33	3.71	2.11	1.01
3.54	2.33	3.77	2.34	0.99
3.54	2.33	3.38	2.34	0.98
3.54	2.33	2.20	2.33	0.90
3.54	2.33	2.20	2.34	0.89
3.54	2.33	2.00	2.33	0.88
3.54	2.33	1.99	2.35	0.97

Save this information as WEEK3.

4. Import data for week 2 from the spreadsheet WEEK2 into the appropriate place in the spreadsheet TEMP.
5. Import data for week 3 from the spreadsheet WEEK3 into the appropriate place in the spreadsheet TEMP.
6. Using appropriate formulas and replication, set up the following information for each company:
    (*a*) The maximum, minimum and average price for each week.
    (*b*) The week change (the difference between the price on the first day of the week and the last day of the week).
    (*c*) Finally, the three-week data, which should show the maximum, minimum, average and change in share prices for the three-week period.
7. Produce a print-out of the three-week information only, in report form, using an appropriate heading and a footer containing your name.
8. Produce a line graph for each day for AIB from 1 January to 14 January (the x axis will be the dates and the y axis will be the value of the shares).
9. Produce a bar graph of CRH share prices for each day from 14 January to 21 January.
10. Save the final spreadsheet as SHARES, and produce a print-out of the entire spreadsheet.

Section 3

Advanced Level

The model—explanation

This is again an extension of the previous invoice model. It allows for more detail and is more realistic, and the design features are also more flexible.

The following different features are allowed:

- Check-digit verification of the customer account number
- Automatic data entry of most data using the 'lookup' feature
- Automatic date entry
- Protected cells
- Full catalogue details

CREATING THE MODEL

Several good design features have been incorporated into this model.

1. Today's date will automatically come up in the date cell. The 'today' function is used. However, the cell must be formatted to show date format (**/rdf**).

2. A catalogue of prices and descriptions is used so that the information can be looked up. Product number 0 is also shown as a dummy product where no products are required on a line. Make sure you enter a *space* in cells B55, C55 and E55 to ensure that blank lines are shown when a zero is entered as product number on the invoice.

3. The description, unit price and VAT code are looked up by the model.

4. A ***check digit*** is used to confirm the validity of a customer account number. This is done by means of a ***modulus***, which is a number that the account number is divided by in order to find the remainder. Modulus 11 is used here: this means that you divide the number by 11 and find the remainder; for example, modulus 11 of 59 is 5, remainder 4. A valid account number is one that has a modulus 11 remainder of 0 when the digits are multiplied by their weights (i.e. five digits would be multiplied by 5, 4, 3, 2, and 1, respectively) and the results added together; for example:
(*a*) Account number: 32154

$$(3 \times 5) + (2 \times 4) + (1 \times 3) + (5 \times 2) + (4 \times 1) = 40$$

modulus 11 of 40 = 3, remainder 7; the number is not valid.
(*b*) Account number: 42145

$$(4 \times 5) + (2 \times 4) + (1 \times 3) + (4 \times 2) + (5 \times 1) = 44$$

modulus 11 of 44 = 4, remainder 0; the number is valid.

5. The entire model should be protected (**/wgfp**), except the data entry cells (**/rfu**). The data entry cells include name and address of customer, account number, VAT rates, and, for each line, part number and quantity required only.

	A	B	C	D	E	F	G	H
1	INVOICE							
2								
3								
4								
5								
6								
7		J. Murphy Ltd			To	Frames Ltd		
8	Customer	12 Castle Drive				21 Arklow Road		
9		Arklow, Co Wicklow				Wicklow		
10	account no							
11	(one digit per line)							
12								
13								
14		3 Date		27 Apr 1994	Order no	Invoice no		
15		4			342	654		
16		5						
17	A/c no status	6	Valid		VAT cat. B	VAT cat. A	Sale type	
18					0.125	0.16	Cash	
19								
20	Part no	Description	Unit	Unit price	Quantity	VAT code	Goods @ 12.5	Goods @ 16.5
21	3333	2 kg hammer, steel handle	per item	7.99			0.00	0.00
22	3456	Paintbrush, 100 mm	per item	1.40	23.00	C	0.00	183.77
23	1233	No 5 wood screws	per box	1.99	31.00	C	0.00	43.40
24	4425	Paintbrush, 100 mm, pure bristle	per item	1.99	5.00	B	9.95	0.00
25					100.00	C	0.00	199.00
26							0.00	0.00
27							0.00	0.00
28							0.00	0.00
29							0.00	0.00
30				Subtotal			9.95	426.17
31				Discount	0.02		0.20	8.52
32				Net value			9.75	417.65
33				VAT @ 12.5 and 16.5%			1.22	66.82
34				Totals			10.97	484.47
35								
36								
37				TOTAL DUE			495.44	
38								
39								
40								
41								
42	Checking routine							
43								
44		15						
45		12						
46		10						
47		6						
48		55		0				
49								
50								
51			Catalogue of products					
52								
53								
54	Product no	Description	Unit	Unit price	VAT cat			
55	1233	No. 5 wood screws	per box	1.99	B			
56	1345	No. 6 wood screws	per box	2.89	B			
57	1678	No. 7 wood screws	per box	3.99	B			
58	1998	No. 8 wood screws	per box	4.77	B			
59	2345	2 kg hammer, wooden handle	per item	5.5	C			
60	2776	2 kg hammer, steel handle	per item	7.99	C			
61	3456	Paintbrush, 50 mm	per item	1.2	C			
62	3333	Paintbrush, 100 mm	per item	1.4	C			
63	3567	Paintbrush, 50 mm, pure bristle	per item	1.8	C			
64	4324	Paintbrush, 100 mm, pure bristle	per item	1.99	C			
65	4556	Gloss paint	per litre	4.98	B			
66	5666	Matt paint	per litre	5.99	B			
67	5998	White spirit	per litre	2.22	B			
68								

Catalogue of Products

	A	B	C	D	E	F	G	H
1	INVOICE							
2								
3		J. Murphy Ltd						
4		12 Castle Drive						
5		Arklow, Co. Wicklow			To:	Frames Ltd		
6						21 Arklow Rd		
7						Wicklow		
8								
9	Customer							
10	account no.							
11	(one digit per line)							
12		Date		Order no.		Invoice no.		
13		=TODAY()		342		654		
14								
15								
16								
17	A/C no. status:	=IF(E4B=0,"Valid","Invalid")				VAT cat. B	VAT cat. A	Sale type
18						0.125	0.16	Cash
19	Part no.	Description	Unit	Unit price	Quantity	VAT code		
20							Goods @ 12.5	Goods @ 16.5
21	3333	=VLOOKUP(A21,A$55:$E$67,2)	=VLOOKUP(A21,A$55:$E$67,3)	=VLOOKUP(A21,A$55:$E$67,4)	23	=VLOOKUP(A21,A$55:$E$67,5)	=IF(F21="b",D21*E21,0)	=IF(F21="c",D21*E21,0)
22	3456	=VLOOKUP(A22,A$55:$E$67,2)	=VLOOKUP(A22,A$55:$E$67,3)	=VLOOKUP(A22,A$55:$E$67,4)	31	=VLOOKUP(A22,A$55:$E$67,5)	=IF(F22="b",D22*E22,0)	=IF(F22="c",D22*E22,0)
23	1233	=VLOOKUP(A23,A$55:$E$67,2)	=VLOOKUP(A23,A$55:$E$67,3)	=VLOOKUP(A23,A$55:$E$67,4)	5	=VLOOKUP(A23,A$55:$E$67,5)	=IF(F23="b",D23*E23,0)	=IF(F23="c",D23*E23,0)
24	4425	=VLOOKUP(A24,A$55:$E$67,2)	=VLOOKUP(A24,A$55:$E$67,3)	=VLOOKUP(A24,A$55:$E$67,4)	100	=VLOOKUP(A24,A$55:$E$67,5)	=IF(F24="b",D24*E24,0)	=IF(F24="c",D24*E24,0)
25							=IF(F25="b",D25*E25,0)	=IF(F25="c",D25*E25,0)
26							=IF(F26="b",D26*E26,0)	=IF(F26="c",D26*E26,0)
27							=IF(F27="b",D27*E27,0)	=IF(F27="c",D27*E27,0)
28							=IF(F28="b",D28*E28,0)	=IF(F28="c",D28*E28,0)
29						Subtotal	=SUM(G21:G29)	=SUM(H21:H28)
30						Discount	0.02	=G30*0.02	=H30*0.02
31								
32						Net value	=G30-G31	=H30-H31
33						VAT @ 12.5	=G33*E15	=H33*E15
34						Totals	=SUM(G33:G34)	=SUM(H33:H34)
35								
36						TOTAL DUE	=G35+H35	
37							**********	
38								
39								
40								
41								
42	Checking routine							
43	=A12*5							
44	=A13*4							
45	=A14*3							
46	=A15*2							
47	=A16*1							
48	=SUM(A43:A47)	=MOD(A48,11)						
49								
50					Catalogue of products			Catalogue of
51								
52								
53								
54	Product no.	Description	Unit	Unit price	VAT cat.			
55	1233	No. 5 wood screws	per box	1.99	B			
56	1345	No. 6 wood screws	per box	2.89	B			
57	1678	No. 7 wood screws	per box	3.99	B			
58	1998	No. 8 wood screws	per box	4.77	B			
59	2145	2 kg hammer, wooden handle	per item	5.5	C			
60	2776	2 kg hammer, steel handle	per item	7.99	C			
61	3456	Paintbrush, 50 mm	per item	1.2	C			
62	3333	Paintbrush, 100 mm	per item	1.4	C			
63	3567	Paintbrush, 50 mm, pure bristle	per item	1.8	C			
64	4324	Paintbrush, 100 mm, pure bristle	per item	1.99	C			
65	4556	Gloss paint	per litre	4.98	B			
66	5666	Matt paint	per litre	5.99	B			
67	5998	White spirit	per litre	2.22	B			

Formulas used

In cell B21 the formula is **lookup A21 A55..E68**.

lookup   The vertical look-up function (vertical columns of data for the catalogue).
A21   The cell to look up.
A55..E68   The range for the catalogue data; this range will not change when copied (absolute).
first item   When the part number is found in the catalogue, move one column to the right and pick up the information. The other look-up formulas are very similar.

The checking routine uses a modulus function (**@mod(A48,11)**).

mod   This is the modulus function, which returns the remainder after dividing by 11.
A48   This is the cell containing the number to be divided by 11.
11   This is the modulus number.

A short spreadsheet example is given to accompany this model, which generates a check digit for four-digit numbers. This can be used to generate valid account numbers for invoicing.

	A	B	C	D	E	F	G
1	CHECK DIGIT GENERATOR						
2							
3	Input code			New code		Checked status	
4	(one per line)						
5	3			3		OK	
6		3		3			
7		4		4			
8		7		7			
9			Check digit -	2			
10							
11	Caculation			Checking routine			
12		15		15			
13		12		12			
14		12		12			
15		14		14			
16		53		2			
17		9		55			
18		2		0			
19							

	A	B	C	D	E	F
1	CHECK DIGIT GENERATOR					
2						
3	Input code			New code		Checked status
4	(one per line)					
5	3			=A5		=IF(D18=0,"OK","Problem")
6	3			=A6		
7	4			=A7		
8	7			=A8		
9			Check digit –>	=A18		
10						
11	Caculation			Checking routine		
12	=A5*5			=D5*5		
13	=A6*4			=D6*4		
14	=A7*3			=D7*3		
15	=A8*2			=D8*2		
16	=SUM(A12:A15)			=D9*1		
17	=MOD(A16,11)			=SUM(D12:D16)		
18	=11–A17			=MOD(D17,11)		
19						

Macros

WHAT ARE THEY?

A *macro* (short for 'macro-instruction') is a series of keystrokes that is executed automatically whenever the macro name is typed in. The macro is stored for use at any time.

Simple macros automate procedures such as copying, deleting, formatting, printing, saving, and editing.

CREATING A SIMPLE MACRO (LOTUS 1-2-3)

	A	B	C
1	Macro name	Command	Explanation
2		(keystrokes)	
3	\N	Gerard Morgan~	Enters a name at the current cell
4			
5	\S	/FS	Saves a file under an existing name
6		~	[enter]
7			
8	\W	/WCS	Invokes the worksheet column width
9		12~	Set to 12 [enter]
10			
11	\P	/PPR	Invokes the 'print range' command
12		{?}~	Wait for a range input return
13		G	'Go print' command
14			

1. Make sure the macros are created far across the spreadsheet so that they will not be in the way when you are producing a new spreadsheet.
2. Macros should be well documented. Give the name of the macro in the first column, the command in the second column, and an explanation of the command in the third column.
3. When entering the name of the macro (\S), make sure you use the apostrophe (') to show that it is a label.
4. Macros should be broken up. It is possible to put 240 characters into one cell, but the macro can be very difficult to read.
5. To create the macro in Lotus 1-2-3:
   - /range name create
   - then enter the name of the macro: '\N
   - and enter the range: B101..B101
6. To get the macro to execute, press [alt] and **n** simultaneously. This will give you the name at the current cell. \P is a printing macro, which contains a 'wait for a keystroke' command, {?} (note the use of braces), which will wait for you to enter the range to be printed before it will print.
   To execute any macro, press [alt] and the letter of the macro simultaneously.
7. Leave a blank row between different macros.

More macros

	A	B	C	D	E	F
1	Use [alt]t to test frequency data					
2						
3						
4	Age at last birthday quoted by a sample of students					
5	Age	Frequency	FX			
6		10	4	40		
7		11	28	308		
8		12	7	84		
9		13	43	559		
10		14	3	42		
11		15	10	150		
12		16	1	16		
13	Totals		96	1199		
14						
15		Mean		12.490		
16						
17						
18	Macro	Commands	Explanation			
19	\t	{goto}B6~	Go to cell B6			
20		@int(@rand*50)	Generates a random integer between 1 and 50			
21		/c~	Copy the contents of C6 to ...			
22		c6..c12~	Range B6 to B12			
23						

This macro can be used to generate test data to make sure the spreadsheet is working correctly.

AUTOMATING PROCEDURES

Using the final invoice example, a macro could be used to help the user of the spreadsheet. The first macro (\P) is a macro that will automate the printing of the invoice. The second macro (\C) allows the user to clear the invoice, ready to enter another invoice. These should be placed somewhere away from the main invoice: for example from cell A100 onwards.

	A	B	C
1	Macros	Commands	Explanation
2		(Lotus 1-2-3)	
3	\p	/ppr	Invokes the 'print range' command
4		a1..h41~	Range A1 to H41 [enter]
5		g	Go to print
6			
7	\c	{goto}a21~	Go to cell A21 [enter]
8		0~/c~a21..a28~	Put 0 into A21 and copy it to the range
9		{goto}e21~0~	Go to cell E21 and enter 0
10		/c~e21..e28~	Copy 0 down to cell E28
11		/ree6..e10~	Invokes the 'range erase' command
12		/rec15..d15~	Invokes the 'range erase' command
13		{goto}a15~0~	Go to cell A15 and enter 0
14		{goto}g15~0~	Goto cell G15 and enter 0
15		/rea12..a16~	Invokes the 'range erase' command
16		{home}	Go to cell A1
17			

MACROS TO ACCUMULATE BALANCES

It would be nice to be able to retain certain information on the final invoice example. Cumulative totals of the amounts due and VAT amounts for all invoices would be useful accounting information.

One way of doing this is to use a combination of macros and formulas. When an invoice is complete, the macro will be executed, which will store three figures into a temporary storage area (*named ranges*) and transfer them to the cumulative area, and then the temporary area will be cleared for the next invoice.

The following will be added to the final invoice example:

E	F	G
42	Cumulative due	Cumulative VAT @ 12.5%	Cumulative VAT @ 16.5%
43	**E43+TY1**	**F43+TY2**	**G43+TY3**
44			

The new formulas and macro to transfer totals will require the setting up of named ranges (/range name create).

TY (temporary) — Consists of three cells anywhere away from the invoice sheet (for example the range A200 to A202)
TY1 (temporary location 1) — Consists of one cell in the TY range (for example A200)
TY2 (temporary location 2) — Consists of one cell (for example A201) in the TY range
TY3 (temporary location 3) — Consists of one cell (for example A202) in the TY range

The macro (/A) to do the transfer will be as follows (Lotus 1-2-3):

	A	B	C
1	Macro	Commands	Explanation
2	/A	{goto}g38~	Go to total of invoice
3		/rv~ty1	Copy this value in total to temporary location TY1
4		{goto}g34~	Go to VAT total @ 12.5%
5		/rv~ty2	Copy this value to temporary location TY2
6		{goto}h34~	Go to VAT total @ 16.5%
7		/rv~ty3	Copy this value to temporary location TY3
8		/rety~	Erase all the entries in all temporary locations
9		{home}	Return to A1
10			

This macro should be executed on the completion of each invoice. All cumulatives should then change to reflect the cumulative totals to date for all created invoices.

Statistics example

A spreadsheet can be used to calculate important statistics. The figures given below show the consumption of beer and spirits in a certain region from 1968 to 1978. (All figures are in thousands of litres.)

Year (x)	Spirits (y)	Beer
1968	18	32
1969	19	32
1970	18	33
1971	24	34
1972	21	36
1973	34	55
1974	24	39
1975	29	50
1976	26	44
1977	26	45
1978	21	30

The following statistical information is required from the given information:

- The average consumption of spirits (xav) (**SUM x/n**)
- The average consumption of beer (yav)
- The maximum and the minimum beer and spirit consumption

- The standard deviation for spirits, which is the average change or variation from the average (the formula used to calculate this is **(SUM(x–xav))^2/n)0.5**)
- The standard deviation for beer
- The correlation coefficient—this shows the relationship of spirits to beer. The answer should be a value between 0 and 1 (0.94). If the answer is near to 1, then there is a very strong relationship between spirit consumption and beer consumption (i.e. when one goes up, so does the other). If the answer is 0, there is no relationship. The formula is: **((n*SUM(x*y))–(SUMx*SUMy))/((((n*SUM(x^2))–(SUMx)^2)* ((n*SUM(y^2))–(SUMy)^2))^0.5)**

where x is the number of litres of spirits consumed in each year,
xav is the average number of litres of spirits,
n is the number of numbers (use the 'count' function),
and y is the number of litres of beer consumed in each year.

CREATING THE MODEL

To calculate the correlation coefficient and standard deviation, you will need to set up columns of data. The following columns will be necessary:

(y–yav)^2 for each year, and show the sum of this column to give **SUM(y–yav)^2**
(x–xav)^2 for each year, and show the sum of this column to give **SUM(x–xav)^2**
x*y for each year, and show the sum of this column to give **SUM(x*y)**
x^2 for each year, and show the sum of this column to give **SUM(x^2)**
y^2 for each year, and show the sum of this column to give **SUM(y^2)**

Also, as a means of simplifying the complex correlation coefficient formula, it can be split up into four distinct parts:

(A) **n*SUM(x*y)**
(B) **SUM*SUMy**
(C) **(n*SUM(x^2))–(SUMx)^2**
(D) **(n*SUM(y^2))–(SUMy)^2**

The formulas for calculating steps A to D above can then be entered into separate cells. Finally the correlation coefficient would be calculated using these cells, as follows:

(A–B)/((C*D)^0.5).

	A	B	C	D	E	F	G	H	I
1	CONSUMPTION OF SPIRITS AND BEER, IRELAND, 1968–1978								
2		x	y						
3	Year	Spirits	Beer	(x-xav)^2	x*y	x^2	y^2	(y-yav)^2	
4		(milion litres)							
5	1968	18	32	31.77	576.00	324.00	1024.00	50.28	
6	1969	19	32	21.50	608.00	361.00	1024.00	50.28	
7	1970	18	33	31.77	594.00	324.00	1089.00	37.10	
8	1971	24	34	0.13	816.00	576.00	1156.00	25.92	
9	1972	21	36	6.95	756.00	441.00	1296.00	9.55	
10	1973	34	55	107.40	1870.00	1156.00	3025.00	253.10	
11	1974	24	39	0.13	936.00	576.00	1521.00	0.01	
12	1975	29	50	28.77	1450.00	841.00	2500.00	119.01	
13	1976	26	44	5.59	1144.00	676.00	1936.00	24.10	
14	1977	26	45	5.59	1170.00	676.00	2025.00	34.92	
15	1978	21	30	6.95	630.00	441.00	900.00	82.64	
16		---------	---------	---------	---------	---------	---------	---------	
17	Sums	260	430	246.54545	10550	6392	17496	35374.55	
18		=========	=========	=========	=========	=========	=========	=========	
19	Statistics								
20		x	y						
21	Average	23.64	39.09						
22	Min.	18.00	30.00						
23	Max.	34.00	55.00						
24	Std dev.	4.73	56.71						
25	Corr. coeff.	0.94							
26									
27	(A)	116050							
28	(B)	111800							
29	(C)	2712							
30	(D)	7556							
31	Number of numbers	11							
32									

	A	B	C	D	E	F	G	H	I
1	CONSUMPTION								
2		x	y						
3	Year	Spirits	Beer	(x-xav)^2	x*y	x^2	y^2	(y-yav)^2	
4		(milion litres)							
5	1968	18	32	=(B5-$B$21)	=B5*C5	=B5^2	=C5^2	=(C5-$C$21)	
6	=A5+1	19	32	=(B6-$B$21)	=B6*C6	=B6^2	=C6^2	=(C6-$C$21)	
7	=A6+1	18	33	=(B7-$B$21)	=B7*C7	=B7^2	=C7^2	=(C7-$C$21)	
8	=A7+1	24	34	=(B8-$B$21)	=B8*C8	=B8^2	=C8^2	=(C8-$C$21)	
9	=A8+1	21	36	=(B9-$B$21)	=B9*C9	=B9^2	=C9^2	=(C9-$C$21)	
10	=A9+1	34	55	=(B10-$B$2	=B10*C10	=B10^2	=C10^2	=(C10-$C$21	
11	=A10+1	24	39	=(B11-$B$2	=B11*C11	=B11^2	=C11^2	=(C11-$C$21	
12	=A11+1	29	50	=(B12-$B$2	=B12*C12	=B12^2	=C12^2	=(C12-$C$21	
13	=A12+1	26	44	=(B13-$B$2	=B13*C13	=B13^2	=C13^2	=(C13-$C$2	
14	=A13+1	26	45	=(B14-$B$2	=B14*C14	=B14^2	=C14^2	=(C14-$C$2	
15	=A14+1	21	30	=(B15-$B$2	=B15*C15	=B15^2	=C15^2	=(C15-$C$2	
16		---------	---------	---------	---------	---------	---------	---------	
17	Sums	=SUM(B5:B15)	=SUM(C5:C15)	=SUM(D5:D15	=SUM(E5:E15	=SUM(F5:F15	=SUM(G5:G15	=SUM(B17:G1	
18		=========	=========	=========	=========	=========	=========	=========	
19	Statistics								
20		x	y						
21	Average	=AVERAGE(B5:B15)	=AVERAGE(C5:C15)						
22	Min.	=MIN(B5:B15)	=MIN(C5:C15)						
23	Max.	=MAX(B5:B15)	=MAX(C5:C15)						
24	Std dev.	=(D17/B31)^0.5	=(H17/B31)^0.5						
25	Corr. coeff.	=(B27-B28)/(B29*B30)^0.							
26									
27	(A)	=B31*E17							
28	(B)	=B17*C17							
29	(C)	=((B31*F17)-(B17^2))							
30	(D)	=((B31*G17)-(C17^2))							
31	Number of nur	=COUNTA(B5:B15)							
32									

Spreadsheet assignments—advanced level

FUNCTIONS AND COMMANDS REQUIRED FOR ASSIGNMENTS

These assignments are graded, and you are advised to work through them in the order in which they are presented.

As you progress through the assignments you will discover that in order to carry out an assignment you will need to know (or your tutor will show you) the functions and commands specific to your spreadsheet program. You will also be practising commands and functions learnt in earlier assignments.

Some assignments require that you have some background knowledge of the problem involved in the question. This is indicated under the heading 'Concept understanding'.

ASSIGNMENT 1
—Creating a spreadsheet
—The 'lookup' function
—The 'if' function
—Printing the spreadsheet
—Macro to print and clear
—Sorting data in alphabetical order

ASSIGNMENT 2
Concept understanding: statistical concepts: correlation coefficients, standard deviations, the t test
—Complex formula manipulation
—The standard deviation function
—The multiple-condition 'if' function
—Macro to generate test data
—Line graph

ASSIGNMENT 3
Concept understanding: present value, internal rate of return
—The 'present value' function
—The 'internal rate of return' function
—The multiple-condition 'if' function

ASSIGNMENT 4
Concept understanding: wage analysis
—The 'integer' function
—Sorting alphabetically
—Printing and producing a report sheet

Assignment 5
—The 'lookup' function
—Design and documentation
—Customised menu of macro options
—Sorting numerically

Assignment 6
—The 'if' function
—Macro for producing a report
—Macro for printing and clearing
—Circular calculation
—Macro to cumulate using temporary values

Assignment 1

Compusystems Ltd has five products in its sales range, and they are coded 1 to 5. The spreadsheet is used for order processing and for calculation of amounts due. It also cumulates sales figures for these products.

The following are the prices, costs and model description of the computer products on sale:

Code	1	2	3	4	5
Price	£3,000	£1,500	£1,000	£700	£580
Cost	£2,000	£1,000	£800	£500	£400
Model	PC 486-80	PC 386-80	PC 386-60	PC 286-60	PC 286-40

The following orders have been received:

Customer	Product code	Quantity
Compu-Add	1	20
Defcom	5	10
QTH	5	15
Peat's	3	8
Digital	2	4
Micro-AT	1	14
Compuscene	4	22
Moss	2	10
Microsoft	3	10

The following information needs to be shown for *each* customer:

Model type: Use 'lookup'.
First price: Price × quantity ordered (use 'lookup').
Discount: Fifteen or more units ordered, 10 per cent discount on first price; fewer than fifteen units ordered, no discount.

Total cost: Cost × quantity ordered (use 'lookup').
VAT: Calculated as 25 per cent of first price less discount.
Total due: First price less discount, plus VAT.
Sales analysis: Five analysis columns are required, one for each product. These columns cumulate the 'total due' for products 1 to 5; for example, if all the orders were for product 1, then only the product 1 analysis column would have numbers in it (use the 'if' function). Show the total for each of the analysis columns.

The only inputs by the user are customer name, product codes, and quantity ordered. All other calculations should be done automatically by the program.

1. Set up the spreadsheet, entering the above data for each order, and show the required information, using the appropriate formulas and replication.
2. Show in an appropriate area of the spreadsheet the average amount due for the nine customers above.
3. Insert a new column to show the actual date of each order. Make sure the cell is in date format.

   The dates are as follows (the first date is for an order from Compu-Add):

   > 12/01/93
   > 14/01/93
   > 19/01/93
   > 2/02/93
   > 4/02/93
   > 4/02/93
   > 4/02/93
   > 21/02/93
   > 1/03/93

4. Show in an appropriate area of the spreadsheet (using suitable headings) the total profit (the first price less discounts and total costs). Create a macro that will print this area only.
5. Sort the list of customers in alphabetical order.
6. Produce a print-out of the entire sheet by means of a single macro.
7. Create a macro to blank out all customer orders for subsequent data entry.
8. Save the sheet as SALES.

Assignment 2

The spreadsheet used earlier for calculating statistics was employed to calculate a correlation coefficient. This answer is often tested using a test called the *t* test.

The test is used to check if this correlation is significant. It involves several stages, as follows:

Step 1. Calculate r^2.
  r = the correlation coefficient; r^2 = (correlation coefficient)^2.

Step 2. Calculate the *t* test value.
  n = number of numbers.

Formula:

$$t \text{ test value (TTV)} = ((r^2 \div (1 - r^2))(n - 2))^{0.5}$$

Step 3. Look up the table value for 99 per cent and 95 per cent confidence level. This is done by looking up $n - 2$ on the top line and looking up the figure for 95 and 99 per cent.

	1	2	3	4	5	6	7	8	9	10	11
95%	12.7	14.3	3.18	2.78	2.57	2.45	2.37	2.31	2.26	2.23	2.2
99%	63.66	9.93	5.84	4.6	4.03	3.71	3.5	3.36	3.25	3.17	3.11

	12	13	14	15	16	17	18	19	20	21	22
95%	2.18	2.16	2.15	2.13	2.12	2.11	2.10	2.09	2.09	2.08	2.07
99%	3.05	3.01	2.98	2.95	2.92	2.90	2.88	2.86	2.85	2.83	2.82

Step 4. *Conclusion.* If the t table value is greater than or equal to the t test value *or* less than or equal to the negative t table value for both 95 and 99 per cent, then the original correlation figure is significant.

EXAMPLE

$r = 0.91$
$n = 8$ (eight numbers in the list)
Step 1. $r^2 = 0.8281$
Step 2. t test value (TTV) $= (((0.8281 \div (1 - 0.8281))(8 - 2))^{0.5}$
$= (28.904)^{0.5}$
$= 5.376$
Step 3. Look up the table for 6 (8 − 2) at 95 and 99 per cent confidence levels.
At 95 per cent: 2.45
At 99 per cent: 0.71
Step 4. *Conclusion.* Compare 5.376 (TTV) with the table values ±2.45 and ±3.71.
5.376 > 2.45 and 5.376 > 3.71, therefore the correlation coefficient is significant.

1. Design a spreadsheet to calculate
   —the standard deviation for x and y
   —the correlation coefficient (the formula is given in the example in this section), using the data given below for the period 1980–1990.
2. The design should carry out a t test automatically on the correlation coefficient, using the 'lookup' and 'if' functions and the t table (given above). This test should clearly indicate whether the correlation coefficient is significant or not.
3. Create a scatter diagram (graph) showing the consumption of spirits on the x axis and of beer on the y axis.

Consumption (thousands of litres) for region 1 for the period 1980–1990:

	x Spirits	y Beer
1980	20	35
1981	22	33
1982	20	34
1983	24	44
1984	22	33
1985	25	45
1986	23	47
1987	26	66
1988	30	60
1989	34	67

4. Save the spreadsheet as DRINK90, and make a report to contain the year column, the spirits data, the beer data, the standard deviation, the correlation coefficient and comment only. Make a print-out of this report, with a footer containing your name and today's date.
5. Set up a test macro that will generate a set of test data for spirits in the range 0–30 and for beer in the range 10–75.

ASSIGNMENT 3

The management of a company are considering the purchase of a new computer system. The initial investment cost is £870,000 (A). The computer is estimated to have a life of seven years, with no scrap value.

The following are the benefits (cash flows) the company has estimated will come about because of this investment:

Year 1	£150,000
Year 2	£220,000
Year 3	£340,000
Year 4	£270,000
Year 5	£200,000
Year 6	£110,000
Year 7	£85,000

The interest rate is 12 per cent. The management now need to know if this investment is worth while.

To assess this investment, the benefits need to be converted to present values, as money has time value. This means that the present value of future benefits must be calculated before assessing any project. The best way of viewing this is to ask the question, 'How much would you invest now to earn £150,000 in one year at 12 per cent?' The figure will be less than £150,000; this will be the present value.

The formula is:
$$\text{Present value} = f \div (1 + i)^n$$
where f is the future value of benefits, i is the present interest rate, and n is the number of years. Or you could use the 'present value' function in your spreadsheet.

To evaluate the investment, the following information is usually calculated:

(a) The present value of the benefits for each of the seven years, using the formula given or the 'present value' function. In this example, this conversion will be as follows:

	Future benefits	Conversion factor $(1 + i)^n$	Present value (future benefits ÷ conversion factor)
Year 1	£150,000	1.12	£133,928
Year 2	£220,000	1.25	£176,000
Year 3	£340,000	1.4	£242,857
Year 4	£270,000	1.57	£171,974
Year 5	£200,000	1.76	£113,636
Year 6	£110,000	1.97	£55,837
Year 7	£85,000	2.2	£38,636

Cumulative present value of benefits: £932,868 (B).

(b) Show the cumulative present value of the benefits (B)

(c) Show the investment assessment amount. Formula:

$$\text{Investment assessment amount (C)} = \text{cumulative present value} - \text{cost of the investment (A)}$$

932,868 − 870,000 = £62,868

(d) Show the return on investment. Formula:

$$\text{Return on investment} = \text{investment assessment amount (C)} \div \text{cost of the investment (A)}$$

62,868 ÷ 870,000 = 7.2%

(e) Show the internal rate of return, which is the rate comparable to the present bank interest rate, using the 'internal rate of return' function if available. For Lotus 1-2-3 users: use the **@IRR(*guess,range*)** formula, where *guess* is any number between 0 and 1 and *range* shows the cost as a minus figure and the benefits as a positive figure. For example, the range in this example will include:

−£87,0000
£150,000
£220,000
£340,000
£270,000
£110,000
£85,000

1. Evaluate the following proposal, using your set-up spreadsheet. Assume that proposals are accepted if they satisfy any two of the following three minimum conditions; the decision to accept or reject a proposal should be automatically calculated and shown on the spreadsheet (use the 'if' function):

(i) the investment assessment amount is greater than £50,000;
(ii) the return on investment is greater than 60 per cent;
(ii) the internal rate of return is greater than 13 per cent (0.13).

Proposal 1. Investment cost of system: £800,000. Benefits over five years:

	£
Year 1	200,000
Year 1	400,000
Year 3	200,000
Year 4	150,000
Year 5	110,000

Interest rate: 10 per cent.

Proposal 2. Investment cost of system: £12,000,000. Benefits over five years:

	£
Year 1	1,800,000
Year 1	2,900,000
Year 3	8,400,000
Year 4	2,000,000
Year 5	910,000

Interest rate: 12.5 per cent.

ASSIGNMENT 4

This spreadsheet allows the wages of individual employees to be broken down into the minimum number of notes and coins required. It also totals the number of notes and coins needed for a particular wage run.

The only entries in this spreadsheet are the employee name and actual net wage. All other figures are automatically calculated by the program.

1. Set up the spreadsheet as given, using the appropriate formulas and replication. Allow for at least twenty employees.

   Hint: To divide, for example, £235 into the minimum number of notes one would go through the following procedure:

   Number of £50 notes = 235 ÷ 50 = 4.7. Find the integer of this number (use the 'int' function for lotus 1-2-3 or the 'trunc' function for Excel). The number of £50 notes issued will be 4.

   Number of £20 notes = 235 − (4 × 50) = 35 ÷ 20. Find the integer of this number. The number of £20 notes issued will be 1.

   Number of £10 notes = last remainder (35) − (1 × 20) = 15 ÷ 10. Find the integer of this number. The number of £10 notes issued will be 1.

   Number of £5 notes = last remainder (15) − (1 × 10) = 5 ÷ 5. Find the integer of this number. The number of £5 notes issued will be 1. (You will need additional columns to calculate the remainders, and these can be put anywhere in the spreadsheet. All should be rounded to three decimal places.)

2. Sort the list of names into alphabetical order.
3. Produce a report suitable for ordering notes and coins from the bank. It should include
   —a heading;
   —the denominations;
   —the number of each denomination required.

   Add a footer with your name, and print the report.
4. Save the spreadsheet as COIN, and make a print-out.

Wage analysis

Name	Amount	£50	£20	£10	£5	£1	50p	20p	10p	5p	2p	1p
Kearney, T.	£256.36	5	0	0	1	1	0	1	1	1	0	1
Maher, R.	£326.59											
Kearney, V.	£260.13											
Horgan, E.	£112.21											
Maher, T.	£211.00											
Maher, D.	£445.70											
Foster, S.	£211.00											
Lynch, W.	£200.00											
Devlin, A.	£567.00											
Byrne, F.	£567.90											
Dalton, W.	£567.87											
Doyle, M.	£567.87											
Slane, M.	£567.87											
Murphy, J.	£260.02											
Leavy, K.	£254.67											
Byrne, L.	£245.23											
Kenny, P.	£456.00											
Page, A.	£343.67											
Morris, F.	£298.09											
Breatnach, S.	£454.21											
Allen, B.	£123.00											
Morgan, F.	£234.00											
Cole, R.	£234.00											
Hanley, T.	£789.00											
Browne, P.	£234.98											
Smith, J.	£234.98											
Bishop, N.	£234.65											
Morgan, R.	£234.90											
Foster, G.	£234.98											
Totals												

ASSIGNMENT 5

A spreadsheet allows a bus company to receive bookings for specific routes. The following information relates to the Dublin–Wexford route:

Stage:	Bray	Wicklow	Arklow	Gorey	Enniscorthy	Wexford
Destination code:	1	2	3	4	5	6
Price:	3	4.50	5.00	7.00	9.00	10.00

The following bookings were received for the 2:00 p.m. journey to Wexford:

Seat no.	Name	Age	Destination code
1A	J. Myers	25	4
1B	S. Myers	10	4
2A	T. Myers	23	4
2B	T. Maguire	44	1
3A	D. Cox	29	6
3B	M. Purcell	29	6
4A	S. Mac Lochlainn	30	3
4B	F. Barry	14	3
5A	N. Gunning	65	2
5B	J. Murphy	6	1
6A	S. Ryan	5	5
6B	P. Ryan	34	5
7A	J. Duffy	10	5
7B	N. Ryan	50	1

1. Design, create, test and document the spreadsheet to show the following information for each passenger:

    (a) The basic price of the ticket. Use the 'lookup' function to look up the destination code and its price. Print or write out the formulas used in this column.

    (b) The destination (use the 'lookup' function).

    (c) Discount amount. If a person travelling is under 12 or over 65 they qualify for a 10 per cent discount on the basic price (use the 'if' function). Print out the formulas used in this column.

    (d) Discounted price. This will show the discount amount subtracted from the basic price for each passenger.

    (e) VAT. This will show the VAT on each ticket. This is calculated as 8 per cent of the basic price.

    (f) Total price. This shows the total ticket price due from each passenger, calculated by deducting the discount and adding the VAT to the basic price.

2. Show in an appropriate way the driver's number. This should be an input that the user enters when setting up the spreadsheet. The driver for this journey is no. 221. Using modulus 11, test the driver's number to see if it is valid.

3. Create a customised menu to allow the user to perform the following five tasks:

Option 1. Clear the spreadsheet for the next journey. This macro will clear the input areas on the spreadsheet, ready for the next journey's data.

Option 2. Destination report. This macro will sort the list of passengers into ascending order of destination code. This will be useful for the driver. It will then print the report, with the heading 'Destination report' and showing the following information only: seat number, passenger name, and destination code (in order).

Option 3. Profit statement. This customised macro will set up a simple profit and loss statement. It will show the total revenue for the bus journey, excluding VAT, given the following expenses. This should be produced as a report and printed.

Wages	60.00
Fuel	40.00
Administration	55.00

Option 4. Save the spreadsheet and exit the program.

Option 5. Make a print-out of the entire spreadsheet.

ASSIGNMENT 6

Set up a spreadsheet that will allow for the preparation of a statement of account using the following general format:

Johnston and Company
14 Abbey Road, Galway
Telephone (091) 752788
Statement no. 1

Send to: [customer name]
[customer address]
Customer no.: [customer code]

Date	Ref.	Details	Debit (+)	Credit (−)	Balance

The details are all held manually at present, on separate invoices, cheques, and credit notes. The spreadsheet should allow the following inputs:

- Customer name
- Customer address
- Statement number
- Balance, if any (enter 0 if there is no balance)

and for each transaction:

- Date of transaction
- Reference, if any
- Details (one of the following: *Goods, Bank, Return*)

The spreadsheet should automatically

—look up the customer's name and address when a customer code is entered and automatically place it into the statement (use a 'lookup' table with names and addresses);
—put the transaction in the appropriate debit (goods only) or credit (bank and returns) column (use the 'if' function);
—calculate the new balance after each transaction;
—produce a debtor's listing report (see sample below) by the use of a macro at the completion of each statement;
—clear and print each statement by use of a macro;
—save and quit by using a macro.

SAMPLE RUN

Produce a statement for each customer from the following transaction list.

Opening balances: D1: 200; D2: 0.

Date	Code	Description	£
1/1/93	D1	Invoice for goods A3	33.76
2/1/93	D2	Invoice for goods A4	33.76
5/1/93	D1	Returns C4	12.50
5/1/93	D2	Received cheque CN5	15.50
7/1/93	D1	Received cheque CN7	70.00
8/1/93	D2	Invoice for goods A33	170.00
18/1/93	D2	Received cheque CN4	100.00
19/1/93	D1	Invoice for goods	45.00

SAMPLE RUN 1

Johnston and Company
14 Abbey Road, Galway
Telephone (091) 752788
Statement no. 1

Send to: J. Murphy
12 Athenry Road
Galway

Customer no.: D1

Date	Ref.	Details	Debit	Credit	Balance
1/1/93		Balance			£200.00
2/1/93	A3	Goods	33.76		£233.76
5/1/93	C4	Returns		12.50	£221.26
7/1/93	CN7	Bank		70.00	£151.26
19/1/93		Goods	45.00		£196.26

Sample Run 2

Johnston and Company
14 Abbey Road, Galway
Telephone (091) 752788
Statement no. 2

Send to: G. Ryan
           34 Oranmore Road
           Galway
Customer no.: D2

Date	Ref.	Details	Debit	Credit	Balance
1/1/93		Balance			0
2/1/93	A4	Goods	33.76		£33.76
5/1/93	C5	Returns		15.50	£18.26
8/1/93	A33	Goods	170.00		£178.26
18/1/93	CN4	Bank		100.00	£78.26

Debtor's Report (after Run 1 and Run 2)

Date	Customer Name	Statement no.	Balance outstanding
19/1/93	J. Murphy	1	£196.26
23/1/93	G. Ryan	2	£78.26
etc.			

1. Produce a statement and the required reports above for each customer, as follows:

Customer code	Customer name and address
D1	J. Murphy
	12 Athenry Road
	Galway
D2	G. Ryan
	34 Oranmore Road
	Galway
D3	F. Ryan
	12 Shop Street
	Galway
D4	G. Teeling
	9 Ormond Lane
	Dublin 1

Opening balances: D1: 200; D2: 0; D3: 350.00; D4: 32.00.

			£
11/1/93	D1	Invoice for goods A3	33.76
11/1/93	D2	Invoice for goods A4	33.76
15/1/93	D3	Returns C4	12.50
15/1/93	D2	Received cheque CN5	15.50
15/1/93	D4	Received cheque CN7	70.00
15/1/93	D2	Invoice for goods A33	170.00
17/1/93	D2	Received cheque CN4	100.00
17/1/93	D1	Invoice for goods	45.00
18/1/93	D4	Invoice A76	67.00
18/1/93	D3	Received cheque CN 27	56.00
18/1/93	D4	Invoice A23	100.00
19/1/93	D1	Returns CN9	20.00
19/1/93	D4	Invoice A56	200.00
20/1/93	D1	Invoice A45	56.00
20/1/93	D2	Received cheque	40.00
21/1/93	D3	Invoice A55	57.00
21/1/93	D4	Returns CN3	11.00
29/1/93	D1	Received cheque	34.00

Appendix 1

Spreadsheet Applications, Comparisons, and Advantages and Disadvantages

FINANCIAL APPLICATIONS

1. Depreciation schedules showing year depreciation, cumulative depreciation, and net book value.
2. Production of invoices and statements.
3. Currency exchange rates, where the various amounts in one currency are entered and the other currency equivalents are displayed.
4. Taxation tables and forms showing PAYE calculations and totals, for example the tax deduction card for an employee.
5. Compound and simple interest schedules for investment evaluations.
6. Loan repayment schedules, including mortgage repayments, showing the best options and tax relief.
7. Car financing evaluation, to determine the best option between hire, lease and hire-purchase for a given set of mileage and time variables.

NON-FINANCIAL APPLICATIONS

1. Records of students' marks, including marks for examinations sat and a full statistical analysis for each student, examination, and class.
2. Football league tables.
3. Mathematical evaluations using different mathematical and scientific formulas.

ANALYSIS AND PROJECTION APPLICATIONS

1. Projection of yearly accounts based on predicted increases or decreases.
2. Prediction of future value of investments.
3. Prediction of minimum stocking levels and reorder levels based on past stock and sales records.
4. Statistical analysis of research data, including averages, standard deviations, correlation coefficients, and graphical analysis.

Manual versus computer spreadsheets

Spreadsheets are not a new idea: they have been used for hundreds of years for tabulating calculations. They are usually drawn up on large sheets of paper. Here is a comparison of the main features of manual and computer spreadsheets:

Function	Computer spreadsheet	Manual spreadsheet
Editing	Easy: changes can be made easily during or after the typing in of data by using the 'delete' and other editing functions	Difficult to delete or change data as the data is fixed
Updating	Easy: 'insert', 'add-on' facilities	Can be difficult
Recalculation	Possible: just type in new data	Need to set up a new spreadsheet
Automatic calculation	Possible	Not possible
Extension	Possible; limited by RAM (computer memory) or disk size	Possible; limited by paper size
Replication	Possible, at different levels (relative, absolute)	Not possible
Speed of use	Fast	Slow
When used	Where there is changeable data, i.e. needing regular editing or calculations Where speed of calculation is important Where data is analysed in different locations Most applications	Where very small quantities of data need to be analysed

ADVANTAGES OF COMPUTER SPREADSHEET USE

1. Calculations that would be very repetitive if carried out manually are achieved with greater ease by the facility to copy and replicate formulas.
2. If one item in a spreadsheet is changed, all other figures relating to that figure automatically change. This allows users to experiment with different numbers to test policy or rate changes. These 'what if?' calculations allow better and speedier decision-making.

3. Spreadsheets can easily be edited with the aid of the 'insert', 'delete' and formatting facilities.
4. Many built-in mathematical, statistical and financial functions are available for calculation purposes.
5. Data stored can be quickly accessed.
6. Parts or all of the spreadsheet can be printed.
7. Integrated packages allow spreadsheet information to be transferred into other programs, such as graphics and word-processing programs, for presentation purposes.

LIMITATIONS OF COMPUTER SPREADSHEET USE

1. Care must be taken when replicating a formula, because one mistake in the original formula will result in the same mistake being repeated in all the copied formulas.
2. Computers are costly when used for a single analysis.
3. Staff must be trained to use and program spreadsheets.
4. Only a fraction of the sheet can be seen at one time.

Appendix 2

Good Spreadsheet Design Techniques: a Check-List

- Document the spreadsheet completely.
- 'Dry-run' and test the spreadsheet completely.
- Use built-in functions where possible, including mathematical, statistical, financial, time and date functions.
- Validate input data by using different techniques, such as 'on-error', check digits, and 'if' statements.
- Reduce constant data in formulas; use cell references to refer back to variables in a formula where possible.
- Protect data where appropriate.
- Hide data where it is sensitive or not required to be seen by the user.
- Automate common user operations such as printing, saving and clearing by the use of macros.
- These macros should be well documented.
- Use range names for clarity.
- Graphically represent important numbers.

Appendix 3

Spreadsheets for Fun

Example 1: Magic squares

A magic square is a set of numbers that when added across, down or diagonally will always add up to the same number. This set of numbers is magic for 15.

	A	B	C	D	E
1	MAGIC SQUARE FOR 15				
2	4	9	2	15	
3	3	5	7	15	
4	8	1	6	15	
5	15	15	15		
6					

THE ALL-MAGIC SQUARE

In the magic square above, the numbers were magic only for 15. This time we will set up the square in such a way that it will show magic numbers for many combinations other than 15.

The all-magic spreadsheet will be set up as follows:

	A	B	C	D	E	F
1	Key in a number:					
2		+C4+3	+C4+8	+C4+1	SUM(B2..D2)	
3		+C4+2	+C4+4	+C4+6	@SUM(B3..D3)	
4		+C4+7	+B1	+C4+5	@SUM(B4..D4)	
5	+D2+C3+B4	@SUM(B2..B4)	@SUM(C2..C4)	@SUM(D2..D4)	+B2+C3+D4	
6						
7	This square is magic for +A5					
8						

Now if we change the number in cell B1 to 2, all the other numbers will change, and the square will be magic for the number 18. Experiment with different numbers to see the other magic combinations.

Note that when this number is changed, all other numbers change. This is because all numbers relate to cell C4. Again we can change the number in cell B1—which in turn changes the number in C4—as many times as we like, and the computer will change the numbers automatically.

When cell B1 is changed to 99 we get a magic square for 309:

	A	B	C	D	E
1	Key in a number:	99			
2	102	107	100	309	
3	101	103	105	309	
4	106	99	104	309	
5	309	309	309		
6					
7	This square is magic for 309				
8					

When cell B1 is 20 we get a magic set for 72:

	A	B	C	D	E
1	Key in number:	20			
2	23	28	21	72	
3	22	24	26	72	
4	27	20	25	72	
5	72	72	72		
6					
7	This square is magic for 72				
8					

Example 2: Biorhythms

'Biorhythms' are supposedly a prediction of your physical, emotional and mental states over a period of time. The only input required is your date of birth and today's date. The spreadsheet will indicate highs and lows in all three areas by using equals signs (=). Twenty signs is the highest, and no sign is the lowest. The spreadsheet is given below for 14 September 1980.

A look-up table is used to convert the calculated numbers to equals signs.

You can change the formulas that predict the biorhythms yourself to see if you get some more interesting patterns for a given date of birth.

83

Appendix 4

Graph Types and Examples

PIE CHART

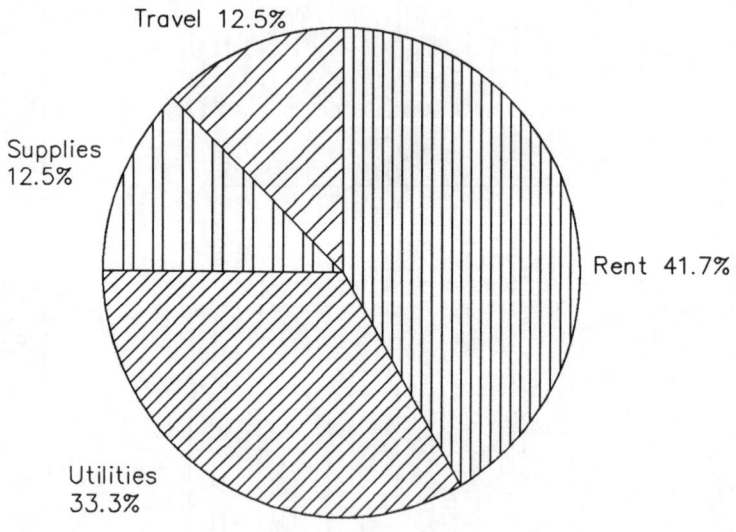

Pie charts show one range of values as percentages of the total. They are used to show the relative sizes of different components.

EXPLODED PIE CHART

An exploded pie chart is one where a 'slice' of the pie is pulled out for emphasis.

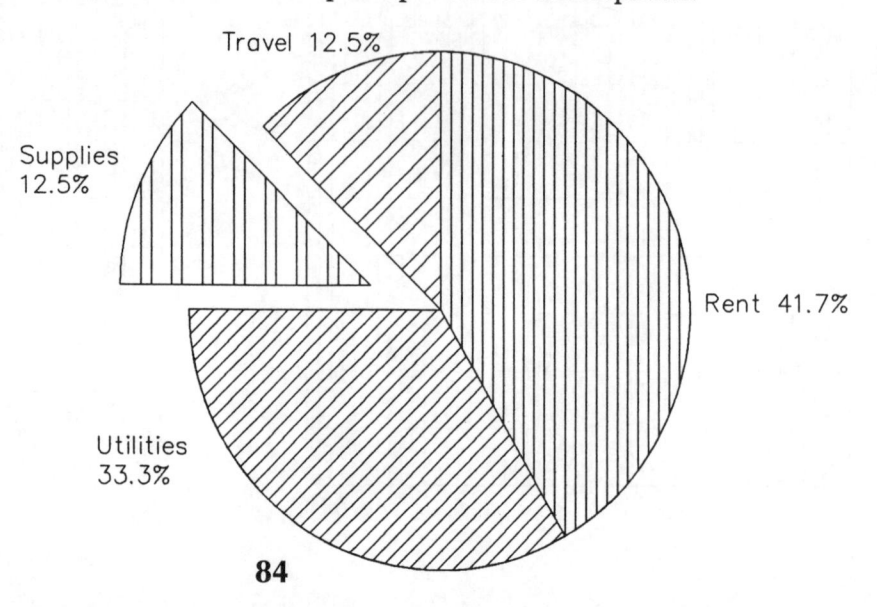

SINGLE BAR CHART

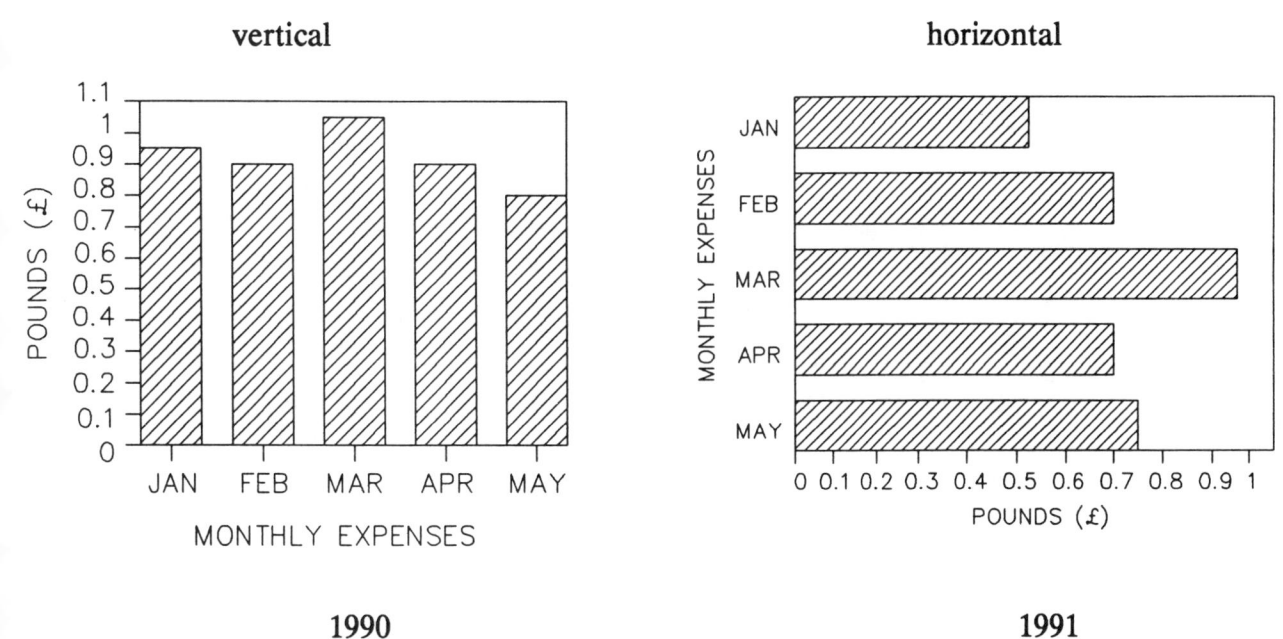

vertical

horizontal

1990

1991

Bar charts show the values of a series as bars of different heights or widths.

STACKED BAR CHART

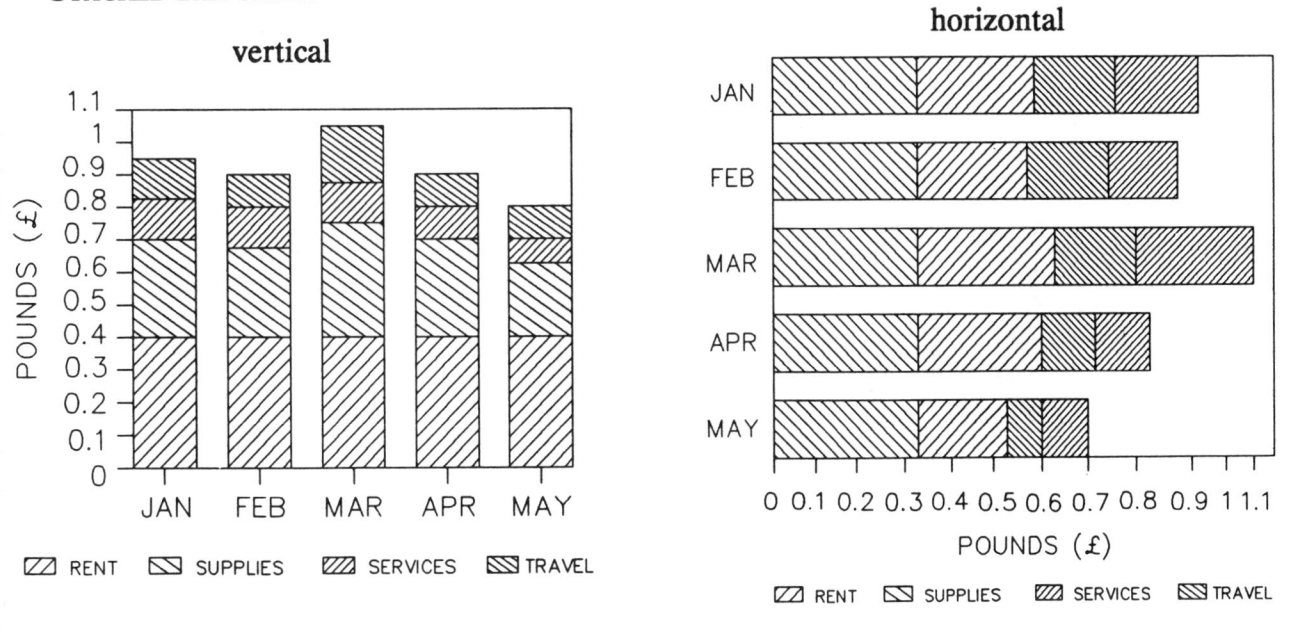

vertical

horizontal

1990

1991

Stacked bar charts are used to show the values of several series of data. The corresponding value for each series is added to the top or side of the bar of the previous series.

MULTIPLE BAR CHART

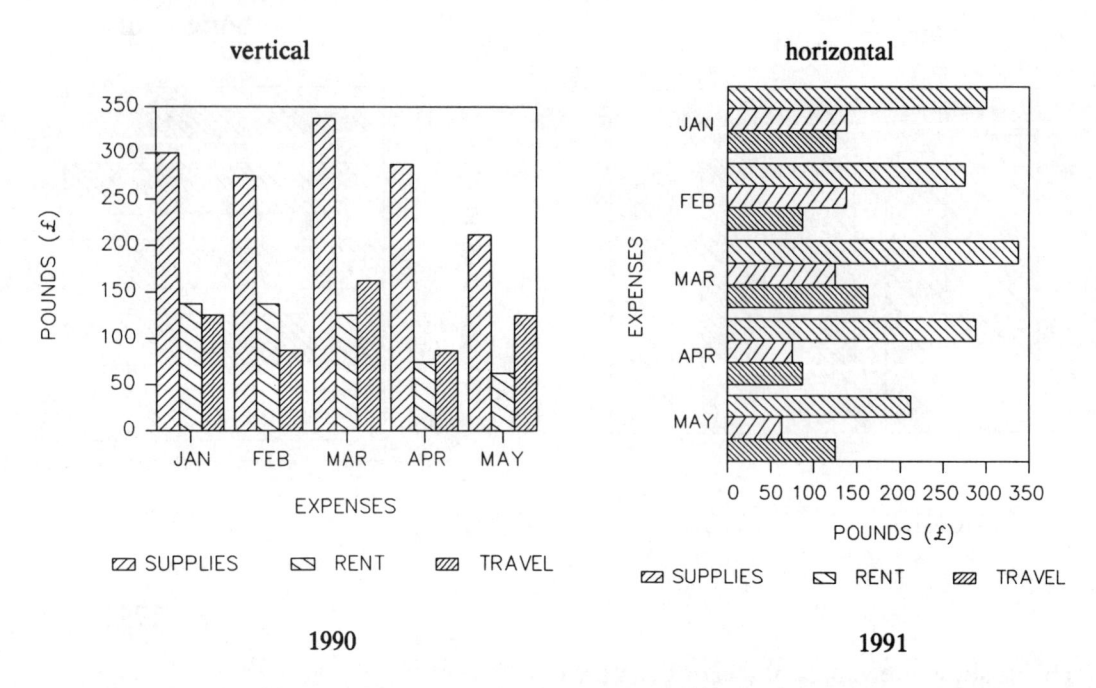

Multiple bar charts are also used to show the values of several series of data. In this case the bars for corresponding values for each series are shown side by side.

LINE GRAPH

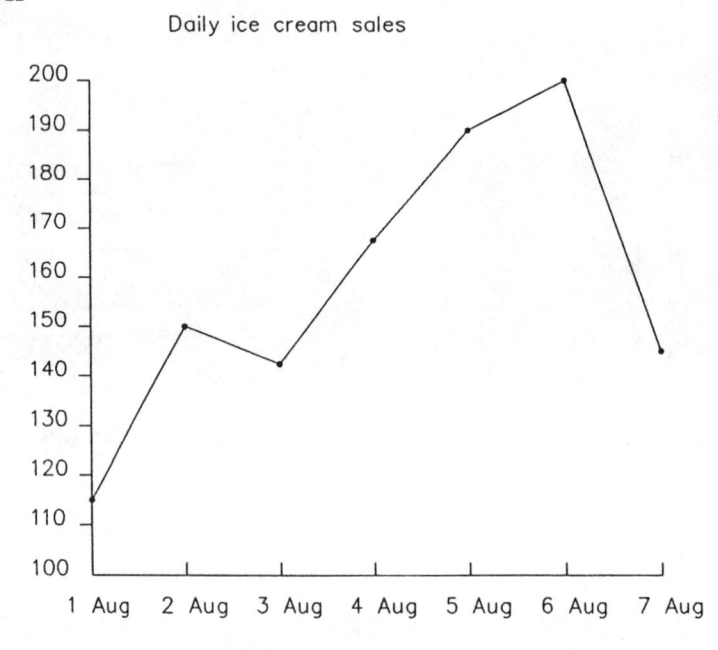

Line graphs show each value as a point above the horizontal axis with a line passing through each point.

86

SCATTER GRAPH

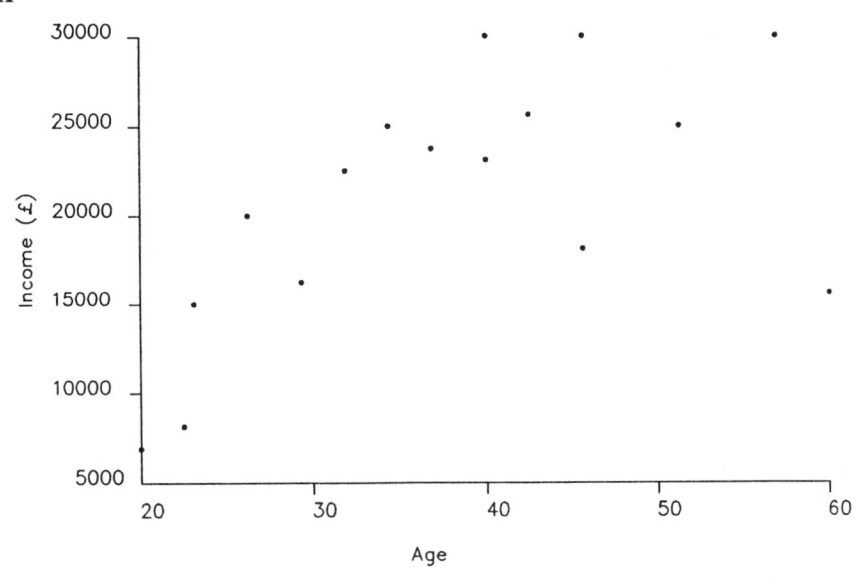

Scatter graphs are used to show the relation between two values. If there is a relation the dots will follow an upward or downward line; if there is no relation the dots will be scattered randomly.

XY GRAPH

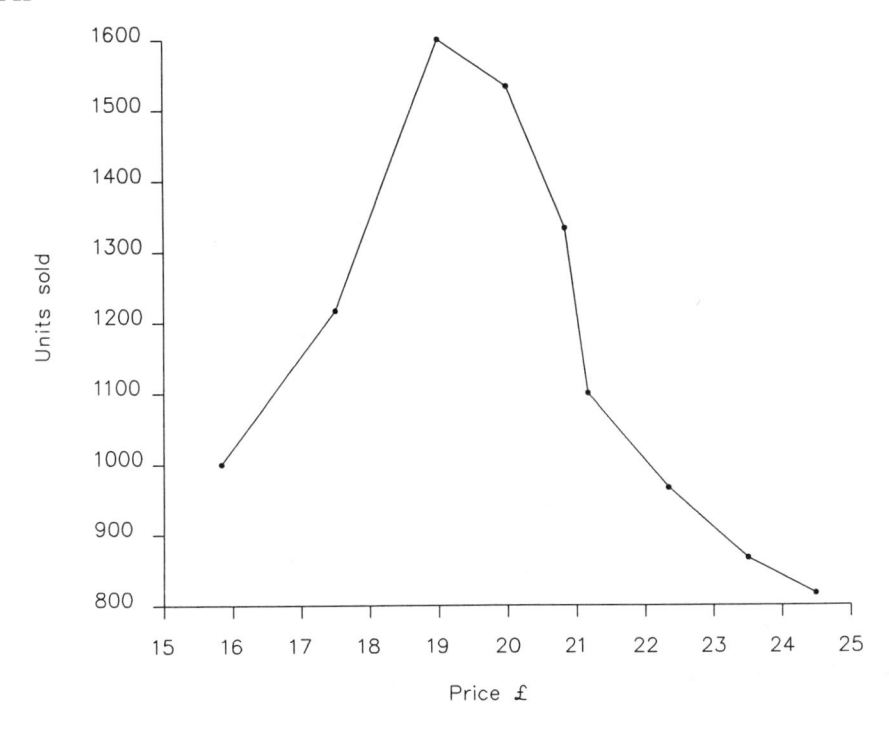

XY graphs show the values of one series against those of another.

Appendix 5

The Information Technology Environment

The aim of this section is to describe ways of minimising risks to the information technology environment.

Definitions

Security of computer systems: 'the establishment and application of safeguards to protect data, software and computer hardware from accidental or malicious modification, destruction, or disclosure' (British Computer Society).

Privacy of computer systems: a part of overall security that involves methods of protecting against unauthorised access or disclosure.

Risks and threats to computer systems

1. Input fraud

This involves entering false or misleading information into a computer system. This is the most common method of fraud, because the majority of users have input access. Examples are:

- the use of 'ghost' or fictitious employees on a payroll system
- the creation of fictitious suppliers
- positive falsification, i.e. where additional data that is false is inserted
- negative falsification, i.e. where data is suppressed (not shown)

2. Alteration of programs

This is less common, as very technical skills are required to alter commercial programs. The most common form of alteration is where a small slice or portion of an account is redirected into a secret account. This is sometimes called 'salami programming'.

3. Output fraud

This is where computer output is suppressed, stolen, or altered. Slow output devices mean that data is sometimes exposed to fraudulent attempts in a data queue.

4. Unauthorised access

5. Computer viruses

These are computer programs designed as a prank or to damage data and that can copy themselves by attaching to other programs.

6. **Physical damage from fire, flood, or break-ins**
7. **Environmental factors such as dust, dampness, and heat**
8. **Power supply cut-off**
9. **Loss of data and programs**
10. **Poor personnel procedures**

Methods of minimising risk

There are three main methods: physical, logical, and procedural.

PHYSICAL METHODS

- Air-conditioned rooms, especially for mainframe computers
- Dust-free rooms
- Controlled-temperature systems
- Back-up power supply (generator)
- Surge controller, to control any variations of power going into computer systems
- High-security locks on computer room doors
- Limited access to keys
- Locks on computers equipment

LOGICAL METHODS

This involves the use of computer programs to minimise risks.

- Non-display passwords can be used for access to programs or data.
- Passwords can be used to limit what the user can do on the system, depending on their job.
- Built-in user monitor programs monitor the activities—such as log-on time, update activities, files read, menus visited, log-off time—of every user of the system. This information is stored for future reference. Printed summaries may be taken of this data at regular intervals.
- Virus protection programs prevent viruses from infecting a computer. An alarm is usually sounded when a virus is present. These programs must be updated regularly to keep up with the many new viruses.
- Virus destruction software enables the user to delete or remove certain viruses if detected on a disk.
- Screen blank programs are time-activated: after a set period of non-activity, the screen will go blank. To reactivate the screen a password may be required.

PROCEDURAL METHODS

Good personnel procedures are important for minimising risks to computer systems.

- Back-up copies of data should be kept and regularly updated. These copies (on disk or tape) should be stored in separate locations in fireproof safes.
- Proper log-out procedure should be adhered to, i.e. the computer should not be switched off before the user has logged out.

- Audit trails should be carried out at regular intervals (twice a year) and also randomly (once or twice yearly). The audit trail will perform a full check on the working of the system, and is particularly useful for detecting input fraud, program alterations, and output fraud.
- Confidential computer output should be shredded if it is no longer required.
- Staff should sign for copies of important documents.
- Proper care of diskettes:

—store disks in a disk box;
—label disks clearly;
—store disks away from magnetic fields, such as electrical devices;
—never insert a disk in the disk drive before switching on the computer;
—always take a disk out before turning off the computer;
—never take a disk out when the drive is active;
—do not touch the surface of the disk.

- No employee should be put in a situation where there is a conflict of interest, for example a bank employee updating his or her own account.
- Staff must follow legislation regarding data storage, i.e. the Data Protection Act, 1984. The eight principles are as follows:

1. Personal data should be obtained and processed fairly and lawfully.
2. Personal data should only be held for a lawful purpose.
3. Personal data should not be disclosed.
4. Personal data should be adequate, relevant, and not excessive.
5. Personal data should be accurate and kept up to date.
6. Personal data should not be kept longer than necessary.
7. A person is entitled, at reasonable intervals and without undue delay, to find out
   —whether information is held about them and
   —what the content of the information is

   and, where appropriate, can have such data edited or erased.
8. Appropriate measures should be used to limit access to personal data or for the destruction of personal data.
   To ensure adherence to the Act, the following procedures should be followed:
   - Store only essential information
   - Improve the security of data, using the methods outlined above
   - Identify data elements that are sensitive, in particular personal details and monetary data
   - Adopt a policy of regularly updating information
   - Anticipate change: when designing or purchasing new software, ensure that it takes into account expected future changes or that it is flexible

Improving the environment for users—ergonomics

Ergonomics is the study of work environments with a view to improving the comfort of workers and in turn their productivity.

Ergonomic considerations were thought of as luxuries in the past. Today they are no longer a technical matter: it is now a management responsibility, enforceable by law, especially with the coming into force of the Regulations on Display Screen Equipment on 1 January 1993. These regulations have six major requirements:

1. Analysis of work stations

Every employer must perform a suitable and sufficient analysis of work stations to assess the risks they may pose for the health and safety of users. Any risks identified must be reduced. Common risks are

—eye risks (strain and glare);
—musculoskeletal risks (posture);
—mental stress;
—space problems.

An ergonomics check-list can be useful for analysing work stations.

2. Requirements for work stations

These include:
- —adjustable equipment;
- —glare-free work conditions;
- —software suitable for the task.

3. Daily routine for users

Users should, where possible, have a mix of screen-based and non-screen-based work; if this is not possible, it is essential that breaks in work routine are provided.

4. Eyes and eyesight

Users have the right to request an eyesight test at their employer's expense. If it is found that corrective glasses or contact lenses are required for display screen work, the employer is liable for the cost.

5. Provision of training

Users of work stations must be provided with adequate training in the areas of software use and health and safety.

6. Provision of information

Employers are required to ensure that all information available is provided to users of work stations.

The diagram below shows a work station that is ergonomically designed.

- windows should be fitted with adjustable coverings to avoid reflection and glare
- monitors should be as adjustable as possible to suit individual operator
- anti-glare and anti-radiation or low-radiation visors or screens should be used
- 'user friendly' software or software appropriate to the task should be provided
- keyboard should be detachable so as to avoid strain of hands and arms
- footrest should be provided if required by individual operator
- document holder should be arranged to minimise frequent head and eye movements
- local illumination provided where required
- 700mm max (viewing range to screen)
- user should be provided with adequate training
- user should have a mix of screen-based tasks and non-screen-based tasks or regular breaks
- user should be informed of all regulations and work practices dealing with health and safety
- angle to be in range of 70° to 90°
- chair should have fully adjustable seat and backrest
- knee and thigh clearance essential

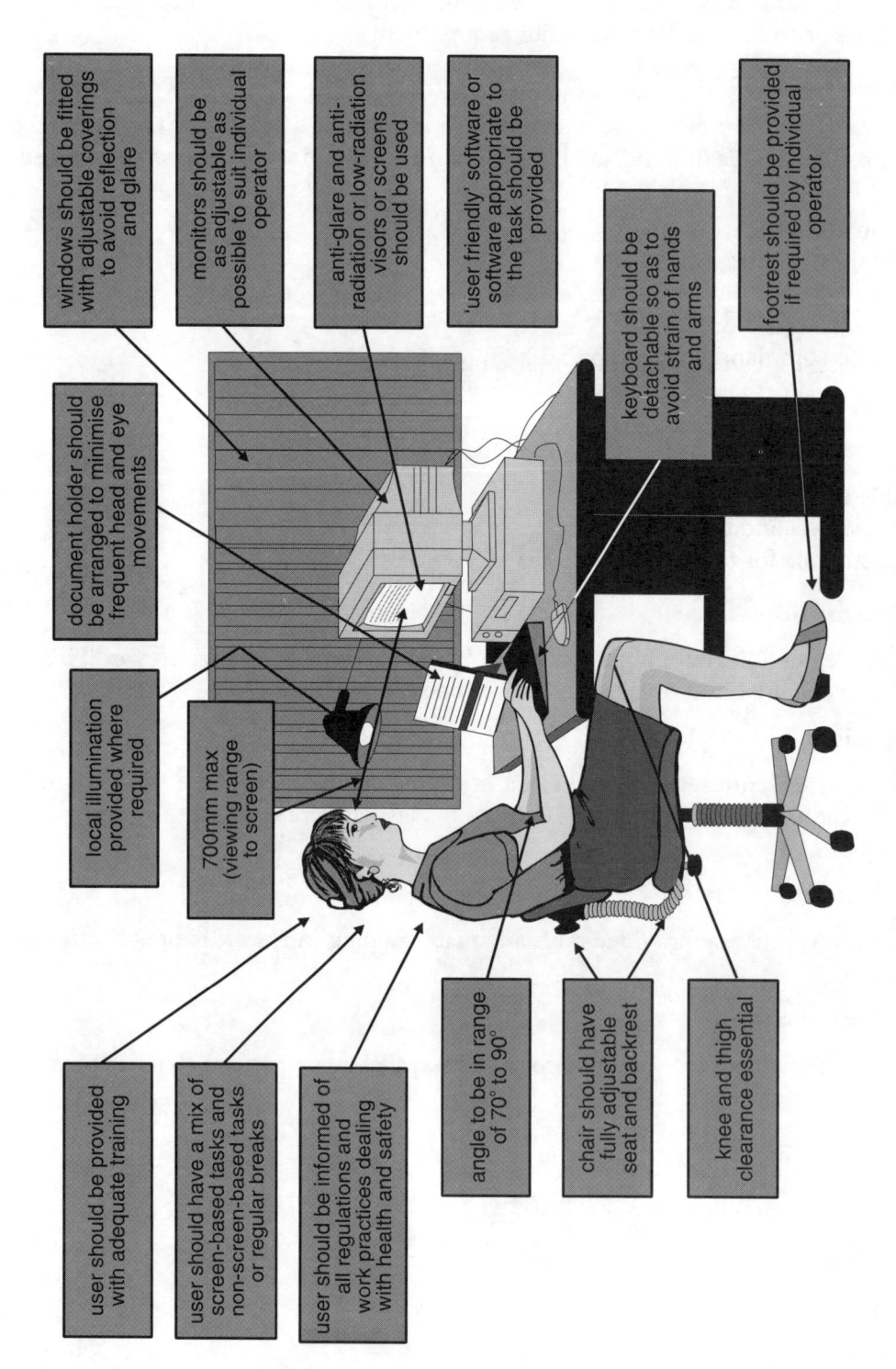

An ergonomically sound work station

92

Appendix 6

Glossary of Spreadsheet Terms

absolute cell reference: a cell reference that does not adjust or change when a formula is copied.

automatic recalculation mode: a mode in which cell values are recalculated every time any cell relating to these values is changed. This mode can be turned off so that only when given the command will the spreadsheet recalculate.

block: a series of adjacent cells usually manipulated as one entity; also called a *range*.

built-in functions: ready-to-use formulas that perform mathematical, statistical and logical calculations, for example @**SUM** (the 'summation' function).

cell: a rectangle formed by the intersection of a row and a column where numbers, labels and formulas can be entered.

cell address: a code used to identify a cell location by specifying the row and column (usually column first), for example A3, B34, Z56.

cell format: the way values and labels are displayed on-screen in a cell. The more common formats for values include cash format, scientific format, and integer format. Common formats for labels include flush right, flush left, centred, and justified.

cell pointer: a rectangular highlight that indicates the position on-screen of the current cell; similar to the function of the cursor.

cell reference: a cell address used in a formula; for example, in @SUM(A1..A10), A1 and A10 are cell references.

cell type: label, value, or formula.

circular calculation: where a formula has a cell reference that includes the same cell as it is in; for example, in cell A1, **+A1+6**. The result of this formula will change if the calculation is performed again.

column: a vertical series of cells running the full length of the spreadsheet. The column is identified by a unique letter or letters.

constant data: input data that changes only occasionally, for example discount rate, VAT rates.

copy: See *replication*.

data entry form: a form used to collect data for input into a spreadsheet.

default: a pre-set value or option that is automatically used by a program unless an alternative setting is provided; for example, columns in Lotus 1-2-3 spreadsheets are by default nine characters wide.

design specification and documentation: detailed data requirements of a spreadsheet application, including input data, output data, formulas, data formats, layout, and data protection. This gives a full explanation of the spreadsheet on paper so that understanding, implementation and modifications are made easier.

fixed titles: a function that allows rows or columns to remain fixed (non-scrolling) on the screen. This function is useful where more than one screenful of data is being used.

footer: a line of information that appears at the bottom of every page.

formula: an algebraic expression using cell references to manipulate data. It defines the relationship between two or more values, for example **+A2+B7**.

hidden data: data that is not visible on the screen. Most spreadsheets allow data to be hidden, such as staff salaries.

input data: data that is entered into a spreadsheet and on which some calculation is performed.

justification: a cell formatting function for labels that allows them to be positioned in a cell to the right, left, or centre.

label: any non-numeric data in the spreadsheet.

macro: a set of saved keystrokes and/or commands that can be executed by a special keystroke or keystrokes.

numeric: any arithmetic value in the spreadsheet.

output data: data that is produced by a spreadsheet by processing input data by means of formulas or commands.

protected data: data that is not changeable by the user; for example, formulas should be protected from users overwriting them by mistake.

range: see *block*.

relative cell reference: when a formula's cell reference is adjusted or changes when the formula is copied to another cell.

replication: the function that allows labels, values and formulas to be copied in a spreadsheet.

rounding error: the difference between the displayed number and the actual number.

row: a horizontal series of cells running across the full width of the spreadsheet. The row is usually identified by a number.

spreadsheet: an electronic analysis sheet composed of rows and columns.

spreadsheet program: the computer program needed to set up the spreadsheet and allow the use of commands, formulas, and special functions.

spreadsheet window: a rectangular on-screen frame that can allow viewing of other parts of the sheet on the same screen.

what-if analysis/calculations: data exploration in which numeric variables are changed to see the effect on the results.

worksheet: see *spreadsheet*.